Eye to Eye

Eye to Eye

SPORTS JOURNALIST
CHRISTINE BRENNAN

Julie K. Rubini

BIOGRAPHIES FOR YOUNG READERS

Ohio University Press
Athens

Ohio University Press, Athens, Ohio 45701
ohioswallow.com
© 2019 by Julie K. Rubini
All rights reserved

To obtain permission to quote, reprint, or otherwise reproduce or distribute
material from Ohio University Press publications, please contact our rights
and permissions department at (740) 593-1154 or (740) 593-4536 (fax).

Printed in the United States of America
Ohio University Press books are printed on acid-free paper ⊗ ™

29 28 27 26 25 24 23 22 21 20 19   5 4 3 2 1

Frontispiece: Christine, rinkside at the 1994 Winter Olympics
Courtesy of Christine Brennan

Library of Congress Cataloging-in-Publication Data

Names: Rubini, Julie, author.
Title: Eye to eye : sports journalist Christine Brennan / Julie K. Rubini.
Description: Athens : Ohio University Press, [2019] | Series: Biographies for
  young readers | Includes bibliographical references.
Identifiers: LCCN 2018058621| ISBN 9780821423745 (hc : alk. paper) | ISBN
  9780821423752 (pb : alk. paper) | ISBN 9780821446645 (PDF)
Subjects: LCSH: Brennan, Christine--Juvenile literature. | Women
  sportswriters--United States--Biography--Juvenile literature. | Women
  sportscasters--United States--Biography--Juvenile literature. |
  Sportswriters--United States--Biography--Juvenile literature. |
  Sportscasters--United States--Biography--Juvenile literature.
Classification: LCC GV742.42.B72 R83 2019 | DDC 070.449796092 [B] --dc23
LC record available at https://lccn.loc.gov/2018058621

Contents

Author's Note

I HAVE KNOWN of Christine Brennan for years. It has been a privilege getting to really know her over the last ten years as our worlds came together in honor of those we loved.

Christine's memoir, *Best Seat in the House,* was published in 2006. My husband, Brad, and I invited her to participate in the children's book festival we founded in memory of our daughter, Claire, that year. Even though we typically feature children's book authors and illustrators at Claire's Day, we thought that since Christine's book was a tribute to her father, we could stretch the requirements. After all, this *is* Christine Brennan. She signed the copy of the book I bought for my husband: *For Brad, A dear friend and a great Dad. Thank you for all you do for the children of Northwest Ohio. Claire would be so proud of her father. Fondly, Chris.*

These three sentences sum Christine up perfectly. Kind. Gracious. Grateful. Empathetic. Christine signed books all day, and when the bookseller ran out of copies, she offered some of her own so that everyone who wanted to buy one would get one. Christine also helped give out our special reading awards in Claire's honor to students. The C.A.R.E. Awards, or Claire's Awards for Reading Excellence, are given to children nominated as the most improved readers in their schools. Every child nominated receives a personalized certificate and a coupon to choose a book from the collection available at Claire's Day.

Researching, writing, and sharing her story has been a blessing. Christine's messages, whether in a note, a phone call, a lecture, or her writings, are consistent. They are always upbeat, down-to-earth, and true to her honest, midwestern roots. She is strong, precise, and humble.

Christine is dedicated to her craft, and just as importantly, to students who wish to follow in her footsteps. She gives countless hours of her time **mentoring** and teaching future journalists. In fact, students can visit Christine's website and find a section just for them, offering her advice.

I've discovered through studying Christine's life journey and career path that she is not only dedicated to getting the story right but committed to teaching others to do the same.

Christine is an inspiration as a journalist, mentor, and human being.

I am honored to share her story.

Eye to Eye

ONE

IN THE LOCKER ROOM

*I grew up in a time where girls were not encouraged
to love or play sports.*
          —Christine Brennan[1]

AUGUST 23, 1980

CHRISTINE BRENNAN had just graduated earlier that spring from Northwestern University with a degree in journalism. All her academic courses and experiences prepared her for this moment. She knew the questions to ask, and the people to pose them to.

Her years as a spectator taught her the game of football. Time spent in the stands following her hometown University of Toledo Rockets or the Northwestern Wildcats helped her learn the ins and outs of the game. She knew about special teams, hurry-up offenses, and illegal procedures. She had knowledge, instinct, and confidence.

That confidence came from her parents, who taught her that it didn't matter that she was a girl. She could do anything she set her mind to.

Now she was a twenty-two-year-old intern with the *Miami Herald*. The sports editor assigned her a story. She was to write a **sidebar** about the visiting football team, the Minnesota Vikings. On this hot night in

1

Miami, Florida, she wore a conservative skirt and blouse. She took an 8½ x 11-inch spiral notebook, instead of a smaller notepad, and a pen.

She was about to make history.

Locker rooms are smelly, often dirty spaces. They are not places you would want to go—unless you wanted to get the immediate reactions from the players and coaches. A locker room is the only place a journalist can ask questions about the contest while emotions are running high, right after a game.

Locker rooms for men's professional sports teams had been considered male-only territory up to this point. *No women allowed.* It didn't matter if you were a sports journalist who just happened to be a woman.

But if a reporter wanted to get the full story, sweat and all, it was where one had to go.

Christine wanted to get the full story. She was going to go into that locker room. *No matter what.*

Just two years before, she would not have been allowed in. There were rules against women being allowed in a men's locker room. But in 1978 a federal judge ruled that male and female reporters should have equal access to both men's and women's locker rooms.

It took several years for the world of professional sports to officially begin to follow this federal rule.

Between 1978 and 1985, since there was no official policy across the board for all National Football League (NFL) teams, it was up to the individual team whether to allow female reporters into the locker room.

So, it was that, in 1980, Christine, the young intern, had every legal right to access the locker room. Yet the world of professional football hadn't fully publicly accepted the decision. Christine was entering territory without defined boundaries. Each NFL team was still making up its own rules as to whether female journalists would be allowed into the locker rooms where the male athletes went immediately after the football games.

The *Miami Herald*'s sports department executive editor, Paul Anger, contacted the Minnesota Vikings to make sure it was okay for Christine to go into the locker room after the game.

2

On this night, the word was out. The locker room for the visiting Minnesota Vikings would be open. And Christine had every intention of going in.

Christine prepared herself for this opportunity. She did her research. She drew upon that confidence her parents encouraged. And she called home to get advice about reporting the story from the locker room from her biggest fan, her father.

"Just keep eye contact at all times, honey," he said.[2]

"This was the first time for me to go into a locker room, and it was the first time for the Vikings to let a female reporter into the locker room. It was quite a moment," she said.[3]

The young reporter was nearly six feet tall. Her height served her well in being able to look directly into big football players' eyes.

The visiting team, the Vikings, beat the Miami Dolphins, 17–10. Reporters gathered in a room outside the locker room to interview the Vikings coach, Bud Grant. Christine was one of them. Slowly the reporters headed into the locker room. Soon it was just Christine and the coach left outside the athletes' changing quarters. After asking him a few questions, she turned toward the locker room.

"You really want to go in there?" Grant asked her.

"Well, I don't want to go in, but I have to go in there to do my job," she said.

"All right then," Grant replied. "Do whatever you have to do."[4]

And so she did, pushing open the door and pushing back restrictions on allowing women in men's locker rooms.

When she stepped into the locker room, she was not prepared for a major challenge she faced.

Since she was the last reporter to enter, most of the players had already taken off their football jerseys. Each jersey has the player's name and number. Christine didn't know who the players were without their shirts on.

It was a preseason game. The names of players were not on the lockers either. Christine had a flip card—a sheet given out by the press box with the players' names and numbers—but it wasn't much help. She wasn't sure how to find the players she wanted to get quotes from.

To add to her dilemma, she heard jeers and hollers from players she could not see in distant corners of the locker room.

They yelled things like, "We don't go in the women's bathroom! What are you doing in here?"[5]

"I was not going to be stopped from doing my job and getting these quotes," Christine recalled.[6]

She was caught between not knowing what to do and not wanting to give up. And she knew better than to look around too much. "I was well aware that this was such a big moment. People would be watching me," she said.

Tom Hannon, a fourth-year safety who used to play for Michigan State, helped her out. Christine knew who he was from years of attending many University of Michigan games while growing up. Michigan State is a huge rival of the University of Michigan Wolverines.

"Who do you need?" he asked.

Hannon pointed her in the direction of the players she wanted to interview. Tommy Kramer, the quarterback, was nearby, putting on a tie. Mark Mullaney, the defensive lineman, was pointed out to her as well. So was another lineman—one parading around without his clothes on.

Christine interviewed Kramer and Mullaney. Then she spoke with the other lineman who seemed to be intent on making her uncomfortable by not bothering to cover up with a towel. Her notebook came in handy. The large 8½ x 11-inch notebook, held a certain way, shielded her eyes from seeing anything of the athlete other than his face and bare chest.

She got her questions answered in just ten minutes. In some ways, it seemed like an eternity. Christine dashed back into the now emptied Orange Bowl and up to the press box with her notes.

She cranked out her story on the Texas Instruments computer as fast as she could. Her **deadline** was only thirty minutes away. She sent her story just in time.

LET THEM WEAR TOWELS

THE DOCUMENTARY *Let Them Wear Towels* features Christine Brennan and other women who made history by being the first females to gain equal access to professional sports locker rooms. An important lawsuit, Melissa Ludtke and Time Inc. vs. Bowie Kuhn, Commissioner of Baseball, occurred in 1978. Ms. Ludtke was a journalist with *Sports Illustrated* and was not allowed into the New York Yankees' locker room. The judge ruled that Ludtke had the right to pursue her profession. Women who were at the center of the issue included Claire Smith of the *Hartford Courant* and *New York Times* and Leslie Visser, who became the first female analyst for the NFL. Even though great strides have been made in allowing equal access to female sportswriters, the issue comes up again every few years. And every time, equality wins.

"It was tough—not embarrassing though," Christine wrote in her diary that night. "Just did my job and got out of the locker room and wrote the story."[7]

A sportswriter was born.

After that, she always took her larger notebook with her into the locker room.

DID YOU KNOW?

There are now over one thousand female sports journalists covering the world of sports.[8]

TWO

DRIVE

I was born a size 6X. I was always tall. Growing up, my dad often told us, "stand up straight, shoulders back. That way people think you are older than you are."

—Christine Brennan[1]

CHRISTINE WAS the first child born to a collegiate athlete who had a tryout with the Chicago Bears football team and a woman who swam Lake Michigan in the summers and played softball and basketball in high school. Her mother, Betty Brennan, worked at home and had a passion for recording life in journals and diaries. Her father, Jim Brennan, was a businessman who loved politics.[2] Either the news or sports constantly blared from their radio or the black-and-white television in their family room.

Christine was destined to grow up to write about either politics or sports.

Jim Brennan was born in Chicago in 1926. During the Great Depression in the 1930s, eight-year-old Jim sold magazines to help his family put food on the table. He threw shot put on the track and field team and played tackle for the football team in high school. Jim re-

Jim and Betty Brennan on their wedding day
Courtesy of Christine Brennan

ceived a football scholarship to Drake University in Des Moines, Iowa. He only played for one season as a lineman before he signed up to serve in the army.

His stint with the army took him to Europe, where he served after World War II. Jim rose to the rank of sergeant, then made his way back home to Chicago. He studied at the University of Chicago before starting his career in business.[3]

He met a bright fellow Chicagoan who attended Loyola Business College. Betty Anderson worked for Illinois Bell, a telephone company, managing clerks, employees who help with administrative tasks like typing letters and answering phone calls. The two connected at a church singles party on a Sunday night. Betty described the day she first laid eyes on Jim as the "best day of my life."[4]

They married in 1955 and moved to Toledo, Ohio, several years later. An opportunity had presented itself. A forklift truck business had opened in Toledo. Jim wanted to be an independent business owner,

Christine with her younger sister, Kate, and her mom
Courtesy of Christine Brennan

and this was his chance. Christine's father sold, leased, rented, and repaired forklift trucks. The business eventually was named Brennan Industrial Truck Company, Inc. As the company grew, so did Jim and Betty's family.

Christine made her appearance in the Brennan lineup on May 14, 1958.

The Brennan team eventually grew to include Christine's younger siblings: Kate, born in November 1959; Jim, in June 1962; and Amy, who arrived in August 1967.

When Christine was just four years old, the World Series of 1962 was being battled between the New York Yankees and the San Francisco Giants. The young family gathered around their black-and-white television to take in the action. Lawrence Peter "Yogi" Berra was the star catcher for the New York Yankees. Yogi was quick and a great handler of pitchers.

Yogi Bear was a favorite cartoon show of little Christine's. Although "Yogi" Berra didn't get his nickname from the cartoon, the names sounded alike to this four-year-old.

As the first game of the New York Yankees broadcast on the Brennans' television, Christine announced to her parents, "Yogi Bear is going to catch. When he gets the ball, he'll steal it, as he does the picnic baskets."[5]

Christine didn't recall this story, but her mother did. Betty kept a baby book for Christine and recorded the whole incident.

At the age of five, Christine wasn't interested in playing with Barbie dolls as her sister Kate did. Instead, she grabbed her father's old baseball glove to play catch with him. And instead of discouraging her, Jim taught his daughter how to throw properly, throwing hard with the motion from behind her right ear. Neither seemed to mind that most dads didn't play sports with their daughters back then.

Several years later, after playing catch all the time with her dad, and hanging with the neighborhood boys playing ball, Christine asked for her own baseball mitt.

Fun with Kate
Courtesy of Christine Brennan

On her eighth birthday, she got her wish. Her dad proudly presented her with a new store-bought Rawlings mitt. Christine held it to her face, inhaling its fresh, leathery smell, just as she saw her friends who were boys do. Baseball smelled like this, she thought.

On the palm of the mitt was a signature, in script. Tony Cloninger was the name on her glove. Christine didn't know who he was. She looked through the sports section of the newspaper to learn about him. She discovered that Tony Cloninger was a right-handed pitcher for the Atlanta Braves. That same year Tony gained fame not for any ball he threw, but for hitting two grand slams in one game against the San Francisco Giants. Two grand slams in one game! And she had his signature right on her glove.[6]

Betty also gave Christine a diary to write in when she was ten years old. Her first entry in the blue-and-green floral print book with the unused lock was dated January 1, 1969.

It read, "Woke up late after staying up last night to wait for the New Year. After lunch, went to the Sports Arena to ice skate. After that,

When she was ten years old, Christine was given a diary by her mother.
Courtesy of Christine Brennan

watched the Rose Bowl and Orange Bowl. In the Rose Bowl, Ohio State won over USC, 27–16. In the Orange Bowl, Penn State won over Kansas, 15–14."[7]

Christine made a promise to herself that she was going to write in it every day. And she did. Even if one day meant that she wrote, "Nothing happened today." And then she turned the page and wrote for the next day's entry, "Nothing happened today either."[8]

The days may have seemed uneventful to young Christine, but there was a lot happening around her. And she was the drive behind a lot of the action.

Christine couldn't wait to grab the sports section from the *Toledo Times, Toledo Blade,* and *Detroit Free Press* that arrived daily at the Brennan home on Barrington Drive. She read all the sports articles, for local as well as national teams.

When she was eleven years old, she'd sit by the radio in the family room, curl up on the sofa, and listen to the Toledo Mud Hens games broadcast from WCWA 1230 AM. With a scorebook her father had given her and a wrinkled and worn copy of the *Blade*'s special preseason section featuring the Mud Hens **roster**, she'd record the game.[9]

Her young imagination got the best of her as she listened to those games, especially the games on the road. Christine sat close to the radio, taking in every sound of those games being played in cities like Syracuse, New York, and Richmond, Virginia. She'd hear the crack of the bat and the crowd cheers, and even thought she heard a man selling hot dogs in the stands.

Christine's father broke the news gently to her that some of the games weren't being broadcast live. They were recreations of the actual game. The announcer sat in the radio studio and produced the appropriate sounds as he read the game plays over a **ticker**. Once she learned this, although she was disappointed, it brought a whole new perspective to this dedicated fan. Christine listened even more closely to the broadcast to determine if the game was live or "fake." Often the soundtrack of crowd noises, which sounded the same regardless of the play, was the giveaway to Christine.[10]

As best as she could, she tried to imagine those games over that little radio. The announcer did not describe the other team's members, what they looked like, or what numbers they wore. If it weren't for her worn and crinkled preseason special section on the Mud Hens, she wouldn't know what her team members looked like, or what number they wore. It was a lesson she carried with her later in life.

And Christine began to practice the lesson in her own sports reports. Christine may have been the youngest sportswriter when she started using her mom's Olympia typewriter to crank out her **previews** of the "Major League Game of the Week" to be shown on NBC on television.

Christine typed up several paragraphs on each game. She placed a piece of copy paper behind the round cylinder of the typewriter, pressed on the appropriate letter keys, and the metal "hammers" instantly printed a letter image on the paper. There was no room for error in typing, so Christine had to be precise.

She had an assistant, her seven-year-old brother, Jim. He'd provide her with all the player **statistics** she needed from the *Blade*. Then she distributed her stories to her dedicated followers: her family members. Christine's first sports writings had a grand circulation of six people.[11]

USA Today, the newspaper that Christine now writes her sports column for, has print circulation of over nine hundred thousand people, per day.[12]

She had to start somewhere.

Christine was hooked on Mud Hens baseball—so much so that she asked her dad if they could go to see the home games, live, from the stadium just twenty minutes from their home. Her dad bought season tickets along the first baseline.

The Mud Hens stadium at the Lucas County Recreation Center was an old horseracing track. The clubhouse, where the team prepared for a game, was separate from the field. Players coming from the locker room and making their way into the baseball park had to walk through an outside corridor. Fans hung out in the space, hoping to get autographs from their favorite players.

The first time Christine and her family went, she asked her dad if they could line up to meet the players as well. He gave his blessing, and soon Christine and her younger siblings zoomed around the players, chasing after all the names she had memorized from her time spent listening to the games on the radio. It was a thrill for them all.[13]

Christine got the bug to watch even more sporting events live, and her dad was happy to fuel her passion. The family went to one or two Detroit Tigers games a year. That's all it took to get Christine and her younger brother, Jim, addicted to following the Tigers. The legendary Ernie Harwell broadcast the games on Detroit's powerhouse radio station, WJR. Many summer nights Jim fell asleep to the sounds of the Tigers games coming to them from Oakland or Anaheim, California, starting at 7 p.m. Pacific Time Zone. It was 10 o'clock Toledo time. Christine often crossed the hall and shut his radio off after Jim had fallen asleep, and her parents did the same for her after she had.[14]

The Brennans on a family bike ride: (*left to right*) Christine, Jim, Kate, Amy, and their dad, Jim

Since they lived nearly in the shadow of the University of Toledo clock tower, the family began taking in the Rockets' football games. Her dad bought season tickets, near the forty-yard line behind the visiting team's bench.

"Dad was the Pied Piper with season tickets," Christine said.[15] Whenever and wherever her father went for a sports contest, Christine and her younger sister and brother were sure to follow.

Along with going to sporting events and school, Christine was still faithfully recording significant events both in her little world and in the big world outside in her diary. And something pretty important was going on with the Brennan family. They moved to the beautiful community of Ottawa Hills, just miles away from their home on Barrington Drive. Although they were further from the Rockets stadium, they still went to each home game.

University of Toledo's undefeated quarterback Chuck Ealey
The University of Toledo

While her mom stayed home with little Amy, Christine and her dad, sister Kate, and brother, Jim, witnessed the magic of the 1969–71 seasons in the Rockets Glass Bowl. With each Rockets score, a Civil War-era cannon shot off from one of the two huge stone towers at the end of the stadium. Under the guidance of quarterback Chuck Ealey, the team scored a lot. And each time the cannon shot off, much to the fans' delight.

The Rockets went undefeated, for all three seasons—thirty-five games in a row, leading to three straight Mid-American Conference championships and three successive winning appearances in the Tangerine Bowl, now called the Citrus Bowl.

"Every ounce of me was being poured into that team, and they never, ever disappointed me," Christine said.[16]

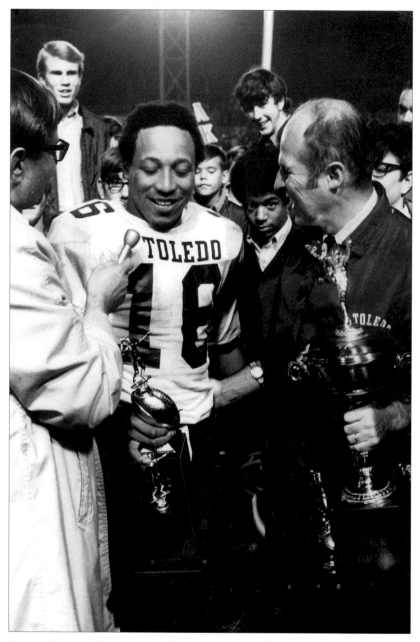

Chuck Ealey and University of Toledo coach Frank Lauterbur receive their medals at the 1969 Tangerine Bowl.

The University of Toledo

A small package sat under the Brennan Christmas tree in 1971. It was for Christine. As she tore off the wrappings, she couldn't believe her eyes. In the box were two tickets to the Toledo Rockets versus the Richmond Spiders at the Tangerine Bowl, in Orlando, Florida, on December 28. Christine and her dad were going to see Chuck Ealey and her beloved Rockets play in the Bowl game![17]

The Rockets won handily, 28–3, led by quarterback Chuck Ealey. It was an exciting victory for Toledo. It also capped a career that opened Christine's young eyes to the injustice and discrimination happening in the National Football League at the time.

Christine credits Chuck Ealey and the University of Toledo Rockets' glorious, undefeated seasons as the reason she ultimately chose to become a sportswriter.

Despite being named First Team All-American by Football News, Second Team All-American by United Press International, and Third Team All-American by Associated Press and in the running for the Heisman Trophy, Chuck Ealey was not drafted to play in the National Football League in 1972.

"Seventeen rounds, 442 players, and Chuck Ealey is not picked. It makes me sad to this day, quite frankly," Christine said.[18]

Christine's dad tried to explain to her that most NFL teams didn't believe black athletes were considered smart enough to lead a team. A childhood friend of Chuck's who went on to play as an outfielder in Major League Baseball, Larry Hisle, said that National Football League owners and coaches apparently felt that, "intellectually, minority quarterbacks didn't have what it took to be able to run the team."[19]

Since Chuck was not destined to play as a quarterback for the National Football League, Chuck's sports agent reached out to the Canadian Football League. The Hamilton, Ontario, Tiger Cats drafted Chuck. Chuck moved to Canada to play for the team, as quarterback.

That first year, his rookie season, Chuck led the team to the Grey Cup, the equivalent of the Super Bowl in the United States. Not only did he lead the team to the game, the Tiger Cats won the Grey Cup. Chuck was named Rookie of the Year and the Grey Cup MVP.

AFRICAN AMERICAN QUARTERBACKS
IN THE NFL

THERE ARE thirty-two teams in the National Football League. In 2017 there were nine black starting quarterbacks. That is just over a quarter of the teams. Progress is being made, though, as in the late 1960s and early 1970s there often was just one African American starting in the position of quarterback in the whole league.

Marlin Briscoe was drafted by the Denver Broncos in 1968, but as a defensive back. He became the first black quarterback to start in a game when he was shifted to quarterback midseason that same year. Many black collegiate quarterbacks opted to play in different positions, simply to have the opportunity to play for the NFL. Chuck Ealey was not one of them; he only wanted to play as quarterback. Several African American quarterbacks opted to do just as Chuck did and played in the quarterback position in the Canadian Football League.

There are a number of up-and-coming black quarterbacks who will be available for the NFL draft in the near future.

Christine played a number of sports while growing up. Due to her height, in the sixth grade a group of boys nicknamed her "Frankie."
Courtesy of Christine Brennan

Chuck is still a hero in the eyes of the University of Toledo fans. He was recently voted as the number one player among the university's All-Century team in honor of the football program's one-hundred-year history.

Just as the Rockets were racking up wins, Christine was chalking up some gains herself. She was growing, taller and taller. She was just eleven years old and was already 5 feet 3½ inches tall and weighed 110 pounds. And she gained a hurtful nickname that year from some of her sixth-grade classmates. "The boys at school have called me Frankie (short for Frankenstein) for some time," she wrote in her diary.[20]

Christine not only kept growing as she entered high school, she also developed the **thick skin** that served her well later in life.

DID YOU KNOW?

Despite his incredibly successful collegiate career, Chuck Ealey is not a member of the College Football Hall of Fame.

THREE

BOX OUT

"This ain't no dress rehearsal."
—Jim Brennan, Christine's dad[1]

C HRISTINE WAS one of the millions glued to their televisions for the 1972 Summer Olympics in Munich, West Germany.

The 1972 Games "etched the Olympics into my soul," Christine said.[2]

What began as a week of competition and celebration suddenly turned into tragedy. Eight Palestinian terrorists entered the Olympic Village and kidnapped eleven members of the Israeli team. Two were murdered during the initial struggle. Christine couldn't bring herself to leave the couch in the living room as the events unfolded outside the Israeli Olympians' dormitory. She chose to spend her last day of summer vacation before entering high school watching the news.

After a daylong **siege,** the captors negotiated a deal. They were to be transported to the airport, along with their hostages. At the airport, an ill-trained West German police force opened fire on the terrorists. Five of the eight Palestinians were killed, as were all nine Israeli athletes, and one police officer.[3]

One of the athletes killed was a man named David Mark Berger. He competed in the **Maccabiah Games** in 1965 and 1969, where he won a gold medal and was chosen to represent Israel in the Olympics.[4] He was just twenty-eight years old on September 6, 1972, the day he was murdered.

It was announced that David was born and raised in Shaker Heights, Ohio, a short distance away from the Brennans' new family home in Ottawa Hills. Christine's mother came out of the kitchen and into the family room when she heard the news.

"Can you imagine what his parents are going through?" her mother said.[5]

The tragedy was beyond understanding for young Christine, especially since a bright young man from Ohio was one of the victims. She tossed and turned all night, and not because the next day was the start of her first year at the high school. Christine couldn't stop thinking about the eleven men killed during the height of their athletic careers. They left their homes to compete in the Olympics, healthy and full of hope. Their loved ones never saw them alive again.

"I couldn't let go of that thought that night," Christine said. "In some ways, I never have."[6]

Through all the coverage of the Olympics, and then all the other sporting news Christine began watching night after night, she noticed something. All of the reporting was done by men. Not a single woman was on camera sharing the latest news in the sports arena. Christine also continued to devour articles on various sports in the newspaper and observed that none of those were written by women either.

"I'd never read a woman's sports **byline,** never saw a woman sportscaster until 1975. She was Phyllis George, former Miss America. If that was what was required, that wasn't going to happen for me," Christine joked.[7]

As she entered high school in 1972, she was still being teased for her height. Christine towered over most of her classmates at nearly five feet ten inches. As tall as she was, it was difficult to even shop for clothes.

Christine hated the thought of going to the mall near their home to shop. Pants were always too short. Clothes and shoes that did fit were designed for older women, not teenagers. Christine got headaches while shopping and wanted to leave the store minutes after entering. Jewelry and makeup weren't her style, other than occasionally wearing blush and lipstick for special occasions. "And let's not even talk about nail polish. I was throwing too many baseballs to worry about that," Christine said.[8]

Christine didn't let the teasing get to her. Just like on the basketball court where a player boxes out an opponent from getting a rebound, Christine did the same with the comments. She turned her back on them, ignored them—as her mother suggested—and didn't let them get to her.

Instead of worrying about her appearance, Christine had better things to do. Like school and sports.

School was first—always first. In the Brennan family, "we were not allowed to get a grade in junior or high school lower than the first letter of our last name," Christine wrote.[9] Christine rarely received marks less than her parents' expectations. As a result, she was very concerned about how her parents, especially her dad, would react to the news that she was getting a D in geometry during her freshman year. Christine couldn't bring herself to tell them how poorly she was doing in the class. When she did finally break the news, she burst into tears.

Her father calmly took Christine into the den, closed the door, and spoke to her quietly about what steps needed to be taken to improve her grade. "For a moment, I thought that I detected just a hint of sympathy in his bright blue eyes. I received the grade associated with our last name in that class the next quarter."[10]

Geometry still wasn't Christine's favorite class. But as soon as she walked into her freshman honors English class, she found a subject she was passionate about and a teacher who inspired her—Mr. Sanzenbacher. When the class read *The Great Gatsby*, he came to school dressed as the main character. During a vocabulary lesson, he once asked a

Christine (*second from left*) was a member of the girls' basketball team at Ottawa Hills High School.

Courtesy of Christine Brennan

student to lie on the floor and wiggle around and get dirty. "None of us would ever forget the definition of the word **sullied**," Christine said.[11]

Mr. Sanzenbacher also taught a journalism class for upperclassmen and served as the advisor for the student newspaper, the *Arrowhead*. Christine and a friend vowed that they would take his class as well as work on the newspaper. Sadly, Mr. Sanzenbacher was no longer at OHHS by the time Christine was a junior. Christine honored Mr. Sanzenbacher's inspiration by moving forward with her goals despite his absence.

Christine's education continued at home as well. Her parents were always teaching lessons about giving to others, patriotism, and current events. The Brennan children were expected to pledge and give their own money to their church and went shopping together every year at Christmas for toys for children who might not receive any.

Christine (*center*) played field hockey at Ottawa Hills High School.
Courtesy of Christine Brennan

On a family vacation to Pearl Harbor in 1974, Christine's dad stood in front of the wall of the memorial above the sunken USS *Arizona*, with all the names of those who died on December 7, 1941, the day of the attack on the American forces by the Japanese during World War II. The rest of the family was ready to take the shuttle boat back to shore. Not her father. He stood there, reading every name and thanking them for their ultimate sacrifice in serving their country.

Until high school, Christine never played on an organized girls' sports team. There simply weren't any. That was about to change. In June 1972, a historic amendment to the United States Department of Education laws was passed. The amendment read, "No person in the United States shall, on the basis of sex, be excluded from participation in, be denied the benefits of, or be subjected to discrimination under any education program or activity receiving Federal financial assistance." This amendment is known simply as Title IX: Title Nine.

Title IX covers many activities, but it is best known for providing more opportunities for young women to participate in sports. Although it was passed in 1972, it took several years for the amendment to be fully put into practice.

At Ottawa Hills High School, Title IX wasn't in full swing until after Christine graduated. Most of the girls' teams played just a handful of matches each season. It wasn't until her junior year that anyone even considered keeping statistics on the players. Equipment for the girls' teams, or the lack thereof, was often an issue. "It was a good thing I liked my jersey because it was the only one I had my freshman and sophomore year. I wore it for basketball, volleyball, and softball, which meant my mother was washing it nearly every night," Christine said.[12]

Christine remembers her field hockey coach having to mow the grass and mark the lines prior to a match and hosting the opposing basketball team for milk and cookies in the home economics room after a home game. A lot has changed in girls' sports since then.

In addition to Title IX, one of the pivotal events leading to this growth was the widely publicized tennis match pitting the women's tennis champion Billie Jean King against former men's champion Bobby Riggs. The "Battle of the Sexes" was held at the monstrous Houston Astrodome on September 20, 1973.

Bobby was chauvinistic: he felt women were less intelligent and not as capable as men, certainly not on the tennis court. Billie Jean believed in equal rights and equal pay for women, including prize money in tennis matches.

Bobby challenged her to a match to determine if women were indeed equal. Tired of his "anti-women" attitude, Billie Jean accepted the challenge.

Christine was among the estimated 48 million Americans who watched their television sets intently as King defeated Riggs handily 6–4, 6–3, 6–3.[13] It was the first time she'd ever seen a woman beat a man at any sport.

The tennis match was about more than just the contest. This was the first time *anyone* had seen anything like this. It was historic, in the world

THE WOMEN'S SPORTS FOUNDATION

BILLIE JEAN KING founded an organization called the Women's Sports Foundation a year after making headlines in her defeat of Bobby Riggs on the tennis court in 1973. The goal of the foundation was to advance the lives of women and girls through sports and physical activity. Their mission today is to create leaders by ensuring girls have access to sports.

The agency provides scholarships to female athletes and supports research. A recent study funded by the organization noted that even though much progress is being made in many areas, media coverage of women's sports still has a long way to go. Of the media outlets included in the study, nearly 75 percent of all coverage is given to the "big three" of men's pro and college football, basketball, and baseball.

The organization also educates and advocates for young women through such programs as the National Girls & Women in Sports Day. The thirtieth annual National Girls & Women in Sports Day was celebrated February 3, 2016, to advocate for and celebrate women and girls in sports.

of sports, in the world of entertainment, and in modern **feminism**—a fight for women's rights based on the equality of men and women.[14]

Years later Christine would see Billie Jean at interviews, Wimbledon competitions, and even at the White House. To this day, when Christine sees Billie Jean, she thanks her for what she meant to her as a fifteen-year-old girl in Toledo. Billie Jean taught Christine and young women around the world they are as intelligent, capable, and important as men.

Christine was learning many lessons as a young woman, from sports heroes, as well as from her own hero closer to home. Christine's dad often told her, "This ain't no dress rehearsal." "What he meant by that was—this is your one shot at life. . . . This is your time to walk on this earth—your only time."[15]

Christine took these words to heart as she filled her days at Ottawa Hills High School. She participated in any sport she could play, kept up her grades under her parents' watch, had many friends, and worked on the student paper as co-editor.

Before she knew it, her time at Ottawa Hills High School was over. And her time at Northwestern University, just outside Chicago, was about to begin.

DID YOU KNOW?

Finally, after forty-four years, the International Olympic Committee officially honored the eleven Olympic athletes (now known as the Munich 11) murdered at the 1972 Olympics with a mourning ceremony two days prior to the opening of the 2016 Summer Olympics in Rio de Janeiro.[15]

FOUR

ROOKIE

"Honey, you're at Northwestern. It's a tough school.
You're a tough kid. You can handle it. Now let's get off
the phone so you can get back to studying."

—Jim Brennan[1]

IN 1976, Christine filled out an application for Northwestern University using the name she was called by those closest to her, Chris. Her father looked at the application and suggested she use her formal, given name. It is because of her dad that she still uses her full name as her byline.

She had visited the campus of Northwestern University for a pre-application interview the fall of her senior year at Ottawa Hills High School. She immediately fell in love. "I was just struck by how gorgeous the campus was, what a beautiful city Evanston was, being on the lake," Christine said.[2]

Christine applied to Northwestern University and nowhere else. She didn't have a backup plan. It had everything she was looking for in a school: A **Big Ten** school. A smaller student body of just 6,500 **undergraduate** students, at the time. Not too far away from home. Northwestern is in Evanston, Illinois, just outside Chicago, and only a four-and-a-half hour drive away from Toledo.

Most important of all, it had a prestigious journalism school, the Medill School of Journalism.

Christine didn't need to apply anywhere else. Northwestern accepted her application. The oldest child of Jim and Betty Brennan was going to accomplish something neither of them had. She was going to attend and graduate from a four-year college program.

On Christine's first night in her dorm in the Foster-Walker complex, she met many students who were just like her: excited to learn and fully embrace the entire college experience.

The *Daily Northwestern*, the campus newspaper, had an open house during Christine's first few days at college. The paper is published by students five days a week throughout the school year. When she walked into the offices, she asked where the sports department was. Christine was surprised to see that the sports editor was Helene Elliott, a senior. "So, women did write and edit sports, I thought," Christine said.[3]

Christine applied to serve as a reporter. Soon after, she got her first assignment. She was to report on the women's intramural flag football games. Christine watched several games on the fields alongside Lake Michigan, the cold winds biting at her. She submitted a several-hundred-word write-up on the games. It never got published. "It wasn't very good. It never ran in the paper. I never asked why."[4]

Christine admired Helene not only for her role as the college paper sports editor, but also because she was writing part-time for the *Chicago Sun-Times* in its sports department. After graduation, the *Sun-Times* hired Helene to write full-time. Helene was proving to a younger Christine that it was possible for a woman to work as a sportswriter.

In 1976, the Internet didn't exist. Christine wasn't aware of Mary Garber, the very first female sportswriter, or any of those who followed, including women who were beginning to make their way onto the sidelines and into the press boxes of professional sports. With Helene, Christine had a mentor, someone who was willing to guide her, right in front of her, showing it was possible for a woman to make a career out of reporting sports.

JOSEPH MEDILL AND THE MEDILL
SCHOOL OF JOURNALISM

WHEN JOSEPH MEDILL arrived in Chicago from Ohio in 1855, he bought a stake in the city newspaper, the *Chicago Daily Tribune*. Along with much of Chicago, the Tribune building was destroyed in the Great Fire of 1871. The newspaper rose from the ashes, as did Medill. He was elected mayor of the city. Under Joseph's leadership, the police and fire departments were rebuilt, and he founded the city's first library.[5]

The Medill School of Journalism was dedicated on Northwestern University's Evanston campus on Feb. 8, 1921. In 1922, the first graduating class from Medill consisted of nine students.

But first things first.

Christine's freshman year started out rocky. Northwestern's academic calendar, like many universities then, was based on ten-week quarters. The school year typically consisted of three quarters: Fall, Winter, and Spring.

Christine had four tough classes her first Fall quarter, including calculus. Instead of writing stories as she dreamed of, Christine was working her way through terms that were unfamiliar to her. **Base. Powers. Exponents.** The professor might just as well have been speaking in a foreign language.

Christine was concerned that she was heading for an unacceptable grade by her dad's standards. Based on her test scores, Christine was earning a grade that was more like the beginning letter in her first name versus the required first letter in her last name. She called home and asked for her dad's advice. He had little sympathy for her. "Study harder," he said.[6]

The exterior of Fisk Hall, the home of Northwestern University's Medill School of Journalism

Roger Mattingly, photographer, Northwestern University Archives

With her first quarter grade point average just 2.75, Christine's dad suggested that if she didn't have at least a 3.0 at the end of her first year, perhaps Northwestern wasn't the place for her.

His threat worked. Christine stepped away from any more sports writing assignments that winter and stepped into the library more often. She earned a 4.0—all A's—the following quarter.

After improving her grades, Christine sailed back into the offices of the *Daily Northwestern.* Due to her dad's interest and influence in politics, Christine was also considering a career in writing about this topic. A friend suggested that she try writing for the paper's off-campus news **bureau**, instead of the sports department.

After nervously entering the bureau offices, Christine was given her first assignment. She was to take two printed articles from UPI wire stories and rewrite them for the newspaper. United Press International, UPI, provided news material to thousands of newspapers, including the *Daily Northwestern*. Students rewrote them in such a way that they would be of interest to their peers. Christine turned the two stories in under deadline that first day. The next day she rewrote four stories. Within her first week, she was overseeing and rewriting all the UPI stories. The following week she had her first byline in the paper.

Christine, the journalist, was on her way. But she had a lot to learn about her craft.

Her first introduction to her formal studies in journalism occurred in the winter of her sophomore year. Basic Writing was the course name. "I was so nervous I almost threw up the first day," Christine said.[7]

The class prepared Christine for fast-paced reporting and immediate deadlines required later in her career. Assignments included leaving the classroom, discovering a story, writing it, then typing it on a manual typewriter and turning the piece in by the end of the class just three hours later. The class put a lot of pressure on students who were, for the most part, not yet twenty years old.

As difficult and stressful as the class was, the assignments also exposed Christine to a variety of stories, including one that introduced her into the world of the Olympics as a reporter. Christine interviewed Northwestern professor Dennis Brutus, who was a South African **expatriate** and poet. Expatriates are people who live outside their native countries. Professor Brutus was an activist, working toward ending **apartheid**, especially in the sports world. Apartheid was a system of discrimination by white people and separation from black people in South Africa.

Professor Brutus witnessed black athletes being turned down for South Africa's international teams. White athletes who were not as good were being chosen over the black athletes. As a result of his efforts and those of members of the South African Sports Association, South Africa was banned from competing in the Olympics due to the country's unwillingness to end apartheid. The ban began in 1964 and was lifted for the 1992 Olympics, after the official end of apartheid.

Christine learned about civil rights and international politics from the professor's perspective during their time together. And she learned that writing about the Olympics was something that interested her.

The class also taught Christine how important it was to NEVER misspell someone's name. *Ever.* This important rule was referred to as the "Medill F", the grade that appeared on a paper if a student broke it. The overall lesson of the rule was to make sure to get everything right in the story. This lesson applies just as much in Christine's writing today as it did when she was a young journalism student. She still triple-checks her work, and often rereads it a fourth time. "It has been ingrained in me that, to this day, I sometimes open my computer to check once again," Christine said.[8]

College broadened Christine's horizons in many other ways as well. Just as her parents had promised, once she left the small village of Ottawa Hills, the world opened up to Christine.

Christine joined Chi Omega sorority, after meeting other young women who enjoyed hanging out and watching football games on Saturdays. Christine also met many young men and was so popular that often she was asked out on two dates in one evening.

The summer after her sophomore year, Christine got her first real job in journalism. She was hired by the *Blade*, Toledo's newspaper, as a **city-desk** intern. Her job? To write obituaries.

Christine took her responsibilities seriously just like everything else she did. "I knew it probably would be the last story ever written about the person, so it had to be perfect. The pressure was on: the *"Medill F"* times ten. Christine began to improve her skills as a reporter, listening closely to the stories family members of the deceased were telling her. She didn't find it **morbid** in the least bit. Nor did her father, who asked which obits she wrote, and made sure to read them first each evening as he sat and read the *Blade.*

Christine's first professional byline occurred that summer, when she was assigned to write a full-length story about a mail carrier who

The staff of the *Daily Northwestern*, 1980. Christine (*front row, third from left*) served as managing editor for the Fall and Winter quarters.
Northwestern University Syllabus Yearbook 1980

was retiring after thirty years. Christine spent all day following Don Busdieker on his last mail route. She asked questions of the mailman and took notes on the stories his customers shared about him. When the paper arrived at the Brennan residence on June 26, 1978, Christine and her parents couldn't wait to see her story prominently featured in the *Blade*'s local news section. Her dad bought extra copies. Neighbors stopped by with their copies of the section. Her parents and their friends were so proud of the budding journalist.

The *Blade* had Christine chasing after and reporting on a variety of stories that summer. Only one of them was a sports story. She was asked to cover the national Quarter Midgets of America auto races at the Lucas County Recreation Center. This sport, for children between the ages of five and sixteen, gets its name from the size of the cars. The race cars are literally a quarter of the size of a car built for adults.

Christine proved her instincts to find a great story in the world of sports, no matter what the competition was. She interviewed a young twelve-year-old racer from California, Jimmy Vasser. He went on years later to become an accomplished Indy Car driver and team owner.

Christine, her parents, and her sister Amy attend Northwestern University's Homecoming game, 1980.

Courtesy of Christine Brennan

Christine ventured back to the sports department every day during her internship. She hung out with and talked to the sportswriters whose bylines she grew up reading; Dave Woolford, Dave Hackenberg, and John Bergener all encouraged her to apply for the sports internship for the following summer.

She did. Christine met with the head of the *Blade*'s internship program before returning to college. Soon after, she received a letter offering her the sports intern position the following summer. "You'll be our first full-time woman sportswriter," she was told.[9]

Christine couldn't wait to write sports stories for the paper back in her hometown. Yet, before that, she had another opportunity through Northwestern's Teaching Newspaper Program. Now known as the Journalism Residency at Medill, more than one hundred media partners, including newspapers, online news sources, magazines, broadcast

Christine's 1980
Northwestern yearbook
photograph
Northwestern University
Syllabus Yearbook 1980

Christine Brennan
Journalism
Toledo, OH

stations, and communication companies offer Northwestern journalism students hands-on opportunities.

Christine landed an internship as a general assignment reporter for the *Lexington Herald*. She covered stories ranging from a visit to the University of Kentucky by a former first lady, Lady Bird Johnson, to interviews with female coal miners.

Christine loved the banter of the characters who worked in the *Herald*'s sports department, and before long, she was attending UK football games and assisting the sportswriters. "Being in the sports department was like being a little kid again," Christine said.[10]

Her love of watching and reporting sports was fueled by her assignments that next summer during her internship back at home. She covered the Glass City Marathon, a NASCAR racing event at the Michigan International Speedway, and the team that made her into the sports enthusiast she still is today, the Toledo Mud Hens. She was thrilled to walk on the historic grounds of the Inverness Club in Toledo and into the press tent during the 1979 US Open golf championship being played there. She saw the names of sportswriting legends at their assigned press seats. Not a single woman was among them.

Christine worked hard, both at her internship and back at Northwestern for her senior year. She was named managing editor of the *Daily Northwestern*, Fall and Winter, overseeing fellow students.

Christine didn't feel that she was the best writer, or the best read. But she always made sure she was one of the best prepared. "I was quick on my feet and loved flying by the seat of my pants when something out of the ordinary happened. I was willing to work harder than anyone else. In journalism, I had already learned that was crucial," Christine said.[11]

Christine made sure to balance her writing assignments with her schoolwork and some just plain fun. As her college career was winding down, Christine was pleasantly surprised to be nominated for the homecoming court her senior year.

And she'd figured out that politics was not what she was going to be reporting on.

The sports world was.

DID YOU KNOW?

There are over sixteen thousand Medill alumni, including Pulitzer Prize-winning authors, a White House news correspondent, national news anchors, and, of course, Christine.

FIVE

UNSPORTSMANLIKE CONDUCT

I didn't for a moment take what he said personally. I had stories to write and deadlines to meet and nothing, absolutely nothing, was going to get in my way.

—Christine Brennan[1]

CHRISTINE LANDED an internship with the *Miami Herald* the summer after graduation, in 1980. Christine learned to stand up for herself, tall and strong, just like her father taught her during a situation with Don Shula, coach of the Miami Dolphins and the "winningest coach" in National Football League history.

Christine's first encounter with Shula didn't go over so well. Christine was sent to the Dolphins training camp to ask about the team's challenges with their running game.

Christine was among a pack of reporters that day. It took her a little while to feel brave enough to ask her question.

"What's wrong with the running game?" she asked.

Coach Shula was sitting on a bench and looked up into the faces of the journalists and cameramen to see who had asked the question. He defended the team's performance. Christine didn't back down. Did they plan on any changes?

He didn't, he responded. And then he stared her down in silence. Christine knew that she had pushed enough. All the other reporters stared at her too.

Christine didn't let Shula's tough response bother her. She stood up tall and straight, just like her dad had instructed her to do so years before.

Shula made sure to wave and smile to her the next time Christine was at training camp. Christine was confused, based on his response to her questioning the team's running game. What Christine didn't know was that a veteran sportswriter spoke up for Christine and told Shula he didn't treat her very well at their first encounter. After that, Shula made an effort to offer more respect to Christine.

"My internship went very well. In fact, the paper flew me to Tampa to interview several of the Buccaneer's players. Newspapers simply didn't fly interns to do interviews back then. Granted, it was just a flight from Miami to Tampa, but it was a flight!" she said.[2]

In February 1981, while finishing her work on her master's degree at Northwestern, Christine received a job offer from the *Miami Herald*. The internship with the paper the summer before helped her get her foot in the door.

Now it was her time to kick that door wide open as the newspaper's *first* full-time female sportswriter.

Several other major newspapers at the time had hired a woman to work in the sports department including the *Los Angeles Times* and the *Chicago Sun Times*. "For the *Miami Herald*, one of the most prestigious newspapers at the time, not to have hired a full-time female sports reporter by 1981 was really surprising," Christine said.[3]

She was just twenty-three years old. The job was a huge step for her, as well as for the newspaper. Her father once again had wonderful advice for Christine. "Don't envision how high the mountain is, just start climbing."[4]

Christine took this to heart. On her very first day, she wasn't thinking so much about her role and assignments. She was more concerned

Charley Pell (*right*), the University of Florida Gators coach, with an assistant coach

about the practical aspects of her new job. "I'm thinking, where was my parking spot and desk?" she said.[5]

Christine's role as the *Herald*'s first full-time female sportswriter was newsworthy. The young journalist found the tables turned as television camera crews came in and interviewed *her*. Christine not only took it in stride but embraced the coverage. "I did the interviews because I always pictured young girls watching and being encouraged. I thought that maybe I could be the role model for them that I never had."[6]

Her **beat** was the University of Florida Gators. It was a big assignment, as this was back when the Miami Dolphins was the *only* professional team in town. It's hard to imagine now, but the Miami Heat, the NBA team, didn't make their debut until 1988; the Marlins, the baseball team, didn't come into existence until 1993; and professional hockey

Charley Pell and the Florida Gators celebrate their 1984 conference victory.
University Photo Archives, George A. Smathers Libraries, University of Florida

hadn't yet made it into Florida. Sports enthusiasts in Miami basically followed football, either the Dolphins or collegiate teams, including the University of Florida Gators. Sportswriters only had these limited sports and teams to cover.

The fact that Christine got the gig did not go unnoticed by her male peers, or by Christine. She knew she was a token: she was hired, in part, because she was female. She might not have gotten the job or the assignment if she was a white male. Christine was hired because the *Miami Herald* wanted a female sportswriter on their staff. Since she was the first, Christine was intent on doing the best she could.

It wasn't easy. Even despite the *Herald*'s push to allow Christine into the Gator's locker room, the coach stood firm.

"So it's 1981, I'm twenty-three, just out of Northwestern. The *Miami Herald* was talking to the Gators, Charley Pell was the coach back then, and they (the team) were saying, 'We don't want her in the locker room.' I had to stand outside."[7]

When Christine showed up, she represented the largest and most **prestigious** newspaper to cover the Gators. She just happened to be female. And she was barred from doing interviews in the locker room.

The *Herald* supported her and kept pressuring for change.

The *Herald* decided to wait out the situation and see what happened. They chose not to file a lawsuit against the Gators, which certainly would happen today if a female journalist was not allowed to interview the athletes in the locker room. "We would monitor the quotes, we would see what other papers had, made sure we were not getting **scooped.** And within half a season, the Gators were saying, 'Come on in and we'll work this out.'"[8]

The staff told her to keep her eyes closed. Christine and team members laughed over the situation. Christine simply took her large notebook with her every time she went into the locker room and did her job.

Christine has maintained that attitude about similar instances over the years. "I tell students to keep a sense of humor. This is not a funny issue. This is about access to your job, but there are moments when you have to smile or laugh, never taking yourself too seriously."

Just as Christine serves as a mentor to students new to the journalism profession, so, too, did Christine have a mentor during her years at the *Miami Herald.*

His name was Shelby Strother, and he worked for the *St. Petersburg Times.* He was a big teddy-bear kind of guy, had a walrus mustache, and wore bright Hawaiian shirts. Back then, newspapers saved money by having their reporters share phones in the press box. The *Times* and the *Herald* shared a phone line. Christine and Shelby worked in close quarters and became good friends.

The first time Christine and Shelby worked together was September 5, 1981. The Miami Hurricanes were playing the University of Florida Gators. More than seventy-four thousand fans filled the Orange Bowl to watch the contest. After the game, reporters were allowed to interview the defeated Gators players in the visiting locker room. It was the same locker room Christine entered a year before to interview the Minnesota Vikings players.

However, the University of Florida was not yet allowing female reporters in. This was not unusual for the times. Just several years before, some teams issued press box **credentials** that said, "No women or children allowed." Sadly, some things still hadn't changed since Mary Garber's years!

Paul Anger, the executive sports editor at the *Herald*, had called the University of Florida Gators the week prior to make sure that Christine would be allowed into the coach's postgame press conference, held down a hallway and past the locker room. On the day of the game though, two state highway patrolmen blocked the entrance to the hallway. Shelby and several other men stood with her in support. If she couldn't go in, they wouldn't go in. Shelby even offered to distract the officers, so the others could rush in. The plot wasn't necessary; the Gators assistant sports information director allowed all of them access to the press conference.

Christine was honored by Shelby's support, and began reading all his articles. She was impressed by his style and learned a lesson: Find people who do what you do well and follow in their footsteps. "Northwestern had taught me how to write news and features with a no-nonsense, get-out-of-the-way, let-the-story-tell-itself style. Flair was not my **forte**. But it was Shelby's."[9]

Christine worked hard to develop her writing style, her "voice," under Shelby's guidance and with the patience of the *Herald*'s sports editors.

As a result of her dedication and tireless efforts, Christine ended up gaining the respect of her peers, athletes, and coaches.

For two years Christine covered the University of Florida Gators for the *Herald*. Then, in 1983 she was assigned to cover the University of Miami Hurricanes for the paper. This new assignment was considered a promotion. The timing couldn't have been better.

Coach Howard Schnellenberger arrived at the University of Miami in Coral Gables in 1979. He boldly predicted that, as the new head coach, he would bring home a National Championship within five years.

SEXISM IN THE LOCKER ROOM

SEXISM IS defined as stereotyping or discrimination, typically against women, based on sex. Simply stated, if a woman is treated as being less capable than a man, sexism is involved. Sexism happened often in Christine's early reporting days. Male athletes were disrespectful to female reporters in ways that would have been totally unacceptable if a male journalist was in the locker room. Christine, along with her female peers, through their professionalism, made a huge impact and difference for current and future women sports journalists. However, sexism still exists today. Hopefully, through continued professionalism and courtesy, as more women enter the field of sports journalism, it won't exist in the future.

It took him just four.

And Christine was there all along the way, witnessing and reporting on the Hurricanes in 1983. It was a magical year for the team. And it was a great year for Christine—except for the challenges one important member of the team gave her.

Coach Schnellenberger allowed her equal access to the players, so Christine was able to get all the scoops on the team. However, Bernie Kosar, the quarterback, often made it difficult for her to do her job. Kosar was a **red-shirt** freshman: he was a sophomore in college, but it was his first year of playing for the team.

The Hurricanes were expected to win only half of their games in 1983. Bernie was young and inexperienced. The season began as predicted. The team lost their first game to the University of Florida. It was their only loss of the season though. After that, they reeled off win after win.

On October 22, the Hurricanes played in Cincinnati. Christine's dad joined her for the game. It rained all day, but that didn't dampen the spirits of the father-daughter pair as they watched the contest. The Hurricanes chalked up another win, beating Cincinnati 17–7.

After the game, one of the Miami players told Christine that the Cincinnati defense was decoding the signals that Kosar used to call the plays. The signals were very complicated, so it seemed impossible that an opponent could figure them out. Coach Schnellenberger denied the claim. Christine asked the Cincinnati coach if they were able to read the Hurricane's signals. He confirmed that they were.

Christine went back to Bernie and asked about the claim by his teammate. He told Christine that Cincinnati was just guessing. She ran with the reports from both teams and wrote a sidebar to her story, sharing what she had learned. The Miami coach was furious over Christine's reporting and Bernie refused to talk to her anymore. Staff from the *Herald* met with the coach. The coach settled down. Bernie still refused to talk to Christine.

At the end of their regular season, the Hurricanes had a 10–1 record. They were ranked fifth in the country and slated to play the Nebraska Cornhuskers in the Orange Bowl. The Nebraska team was tough. The Hurricanes were the **underdog**. The Miami team, led by their young quarterback, was not expected to win.

The Hurricanes got off to a 17–0 lead. The Cornhuskers rallied, but the Hurricanes beat them, 31–30. It was the school's first national championship, and the game is still considered one of the most exciting football contests in collegiate history.

Bernie passed for three hundred yards and two touchdowns. He was recognized as the Most Valuable Player (MVP) for the Orange Bowl. The following year he made team records with his passing and touchdowns. He was named Second Team All-American and came in fourth in the Heisman trophy votes.

But he still didn't talk to Christine. For years, he ignored her, even avoiding her at a small black-tie reception in Washington, DC. Finally, years later, at another fancy affair, Bernie approached Christine and

THE MIAMI HERALD PUBLISHING COMPANY

THE MIRACLE of MIAMI

THE INSIDE STORY OF THE HURRICANES' CHAMPIONSHIP SEASON

CHRISTINE BRENNAN

$3.95

The Miracle of Miami, Christine's first book

apologized for his behavior. Christine accepted his apology, and they had a nice conversation.

Christine's coverage of the championship game for the *Miami Herald*, the newspaper that everyone was reading, led to three new opportunities for her.

One was to have her first book published. Christine wrote *Miracle in Miami* about the phenomenal 1983 Hurricanes season and championship.

Another was to cover the Olympics for the *Herald*. After the football season was over, the newspaper sent her to cover the 1984 Olympics. Christine had let her editor know soon after coming on board with the paper that this was an assignment she wanted.

The third was to eventually cover sports for an even larger newspaper.

An old friend had a hand in this twist of fate.

DID YOU KNOW?

As of 2018 the world of sports journalism is still dominated by males. Over 90 percent of sports editors are males, and over 87 percent of columnists and reporters are men.[10]

SIX

MAJOR LEAGUES

I had no fears or worries covering the NFL in Washington in the 1980s because I believed I was prepared for that role, from my childhood of playing and loving sports to my education at Northwestern to my three years covering football at the Miami Herald *before coming to the* Washington Post.

—Christine Brennan[1]

CHRISTINE GAINED many new fans through her coverage of the Hurricanes during their championship. And her writings caught the eye of an old friend.

Michael Wilbon grew up on the south side of Chicago. Michael figured out when he was seven years old that he would not have a future in math or science. He loved to read and write though and had a talent for creating and tearing sentences apart.

And like Christine, he had a passion for sports. He played every sport of the season with friends in the neighborhood park.

Michael knew by his junior year in high school that he wanted to write about sports and elected to go to Northwestern to major in journalism.

It was at Northwestern that Michael and Christine's friendship began.

Christine and her Northwestern classmate and friend Michael Wilbon
Courtesy of Christine Brennan

Just like Christine, Michael walked into the *Daily Northwestern* offices and told the staff he wanted to write for them. When she began college, Christine was still uncertain about what her focus would be as a journalist, but Michael knew from the start. Sports was what he wanted to write about.

Michael interned at the *Washington Post* for two summers during college, and then he jumped at the chance to work for the paper when they offered him a job covering college sports after graduation.[2]

Michael was in Miami in 1983 reporting on the national championship game between the Miami Hurricanes and the Nebraska Cornhuskers for the *Washington Post*. Impressed by Christine's coverage of the game, Michael took her **clippings** to George Solomon, the sports editor, and recommended he hire Christine. Christine didn't know at the time what Michael had done, or that her name was being discussed in the editorial room of the *Post*.

For now, though, Christine was given a dream opportunity by her current employer, the *Miami Herald*. She was covering the 1984 Olympics! And there, reporting the international sports competition for the *Washington Post*, was her fellow Northwestern grad Michael Wilbon.

Christine nearly had to pinch herself while sitting in the press section in the L.A. Coliseum in July 1984. Christine was at the Olympics, being paid by a major newspaper, the *Herald*, to report on the various competitions. It was a beautiful day. There was no smog, which was unusual for Los Angeles then. She called back home to share her excitement with her parents. Christine's dad was so excited for her that he flew out to Los Angeles, joined by Christine's sister Kate and her husband, Tom.

These Olympic Games were different than most. Many countries were not participating. The Soviet Union led a **boycott** of the 1984 Games as payback for the United States doing the same in 1980. The United States chose not to compete in the 1980 Olympics due to the Soviet Union invading the country of Afghanistan.

So, in Los Angeles four years later, fourteen Eastern Bloc countries, the communist states of Eastern Europe at that time, were not competing in the Olympics. Although this may not seem like a huge number of countries, those who didn't participate represented over half of the gold medals won at the 1976 Olympics.[3]

Christine was exposed to some Olympic firsts during her initial Olympics. The women's marathon competition debuted in the 1984 Olympics. Fifty-six years earlier doctors had claimed that women running 800 meters (half a mile) would become tired too soon! Joan Benoit of the United States took home gold in the 26.2-mile race. Synchronized swimming, rhythmic gymnastics, and a women's cycling road race were also added as new sports.

Outside of the Soviet boycott, the biggest news-making event involved a runner from the United States. Mary Decker was favored to win the 3,000-meter race at the Games in Los Angeles. Also competing

Games of the
XXIIIrd Olympiad
Los Angeles 1984

Jeux de la
XXIIIème Olympiade
Los Angeles 1984

CHRISTINE BRENNAN

MIAMI HERALD

JOURNALIST   USA

∞   4

Christine's press credentials for the 1984 Summer Olympics, her first

Courtesy of Christine Brennan

in the race was Zola Budd, a young runner from South Africa, another country boycotting the 1984 game. Because of the boycott of her country due to apartheid, Zola Budd was running on behalf of Great Britain. Zola also made news for her unique running style. She ran barefoot.

Three laps into the race, with Mary and Zola running side by side, there was a sudden scuffle. Mary fell over off the track, grabbing her legs in pain. Zola turned back and looked but kept on running. As Mary reeled in pain, Zola came to a slow run. The crowds booed at Zola. Had she had intentionally tripped Mary? Zola finished seventh. Neither runner was ever able to escape the tragedy of the incident.

Christine and several other reporters tried to get comments from Mary as she was carried out of the stadium in the arms of her fiancé. Christine didn't hear much. Mary was in tears. Her years of work and practice were dashed in a split second.

Christine loved attending and sharing the news of the Olympics with the *Miami Herald* readers. She told her dad soon after that she hoped never to miss another Olympics. "If a newspaper wouldn't send me, I'd pay my own way. I had found the very best event in sports and I wasn't going to let it go," she said.[4]

Christine has not missed an Olympics since. And she has yet to pay her own way.

The 1984 Olympics were the last that Christine covered for the *Herald*, however. Those editorial room discussions that her friend Michael had started led to the *Washington Post* hiring Christine.

When Christine came on board with the *Post* in September of 1984, she was not thinking about where her parking space and desk were. She was thinking about the significance of working for the prestigious paper. As she walked into the newspaper's fifth floor offices of the *Post*'s headquarters on 15th Street NW in our nation's capital, she felt like she was treading in the footsteps of those who had made journalism history. As she said, it was like walking into the pages of a journalism textbook.

THE IMPACT OF THE
UNITED STATES BOYCOTT
OF THE 1980 OLYMPICS

TWENTY-FIVE YEARS after the decision by the United States to boycott the 1980 Olympics due to the Soviet Union's invasion of Afghanistan, Christine wrote a story about those affected most by the decision.

The athletes.

Since the Olympics only occur every four years, an athlete's dreams of competing at that level can be eliminated due to age and opportunity. Some of these athletes we will never hear about, simply because they missed their moment to shine.

Craig Beardsley, a young man from New Jersey, set the world record in the 200-meter butterfly ten days *after* the 1980 Olympics. His time was a second and a half faster than the man who swam away with the gold at the Olympics.

Kurt Thomas, a gymnast who won five NCAA championships while competing for Indiana State University, was expected to bring home gold at the 1980 Games. He never had the chance.[4]

The intent of the boycott was to pressure the Soviet Union to withdraw from Afghanistan within a month. The boycott was not effective, as the war between the two countries lasted another nine years.

Christine (*standing, second from left*) and fellow journalists attend a press conference held by Joe Gibbs, coach of Washington's NFL team.

Courtesy of Christine Brennan

The staff of the *Post* had revealed many news stories over the years, but none so significant as the **Watergate** scandal, leading to former President Richard Nixon's resignation ten years earlier. Many of the reporters and staff from that time were still working at the *Post*, including Bob Woodward, one of the two investigative reporters who broke the Watergate story.

Several months after being brought on board the newspaper, Christine was assigned to cover the National Football League's Washington Redskins. It was one of the two most desired reporting jobs with the newspaper. The other was the White House beat.

This hiring decision did not sit well with Joe Gibbs, the team's coach. The Redskins, like some other NFL teams, had not been allowing female reporters into the locker room. But in May 1985, the commissioner of the National Football League told the team owners that they must let female sportswriters into their locker rooms.

That July, after driving to Carlisle, Pennsylvania, the training camp for the Redskins, Christine once again found that *she* was the story. Four Washington television stations interviewed her. Her role was breaking news.

Coach Gibbs said that he would obey the new rule, although he still didn't like Christine being in the locker room. Neither did defensive tackle Dave Butz. Dave's huge physical presence was daunting. He stood six-feet-seven-inches tall and weighed over three hundred pounds. Dave often yelled out, "No women in the locker room!" whenever Christine came in to interview the players.[6]

The Redskins organization, led by Coach Gibb's reluctant acceptance of the NFL rules, stood by Christine in her efforts to do her job. Some of the players, including Dave Butz, still made it difficult for her. Once, he was sick with the flu for almost a week before a game against the New York Jets. Dave was so ill that he had been in the hospital and lost twenty pounds, according to Coach Gibbs. He didn't want to miss playing in the game though, so Dave checked himself out of the hospital and suited up. After the game, Christine wanted to verify that he had lost that much weight. Dave wouldn't answer her question, even when she stood right in front of him. "I don't talk to you in the locker room," he said.[7]

Christine didn't want him to get the last laugh in the situation, so *she* did. She saw Frank Herzog, the team's radio announcer, nearby. She asked Frank to ask Dave Butz the question. He did. Dave answered, "I lost about twenty-one." Christine got her answer. She thanked Frank for his help, smiled at Dave, and went off to write her story.

Most of the players' attitudes changed over time. Christine's professionalism, reporting skills, and sense of humor won them over. Dave continued to make difficulties for Christine throughout her three years on the Redskins beat. But, once he learned that one of the other players had given Christine a hard time, Dave stood up for her.

Dave told her that if anyone ever gave her any trouble, to let him know, and he'd take care of him—sort of like what a big brother would say and do.

At the time, Christine thought it was weird, because Dave was always making her job a little more difficult. So, a year later during a phone interview, Christine asked why he said what he had said.

"Because, even if I don't like it that you're in there, you should be treated right when you're there," he said.[8]

The media focused on the issue of female sportswriters in the locker room. In reality, the amount of time Christine spent in the locker room was minimal compared to her time on the sidelines observing and then writing her stories.

During the many seasons she spent covering the Redskins, Christine was often approached to share her knowledge of the team with television stations. She loved being a part of this different form of journalism. It was unlike her experiences as a newspaper reporter. While writing her stories, she often had to file them right away, under the pressure of a deadline. Other times she could take hours editing her thoughts. Television was more immediate, and she found it thrilling.

But writing was always her first love. She continued to use her skills for the *Post* for a total of twelve years. After three spent covering the Redskins, Christine was ready for a different assignment.

The Redskins won the Super Bowl in San Diego, California, on January 31, 1988. Christine flew back to Washington, DC, and switched the warm weather clothes in her suitcase to winter sweaters. She left a few days later for Calgary, Canada, the site of the Winter Olympics.

Christine was on her way to fulfilling her dream of continuing to cover the Olympics—and to witnessing one of the scariest moments of her journalism career.

DID YOU KNOW?

The first modern Olympics was held in Athens, Greece, in 1896. Male athletes from fourteen countries competed in a variety of contests. Women began participating four years later at the Games held in Paris. Any guess as to what sports?
Lawn Tennis and Golf.

SEVEN

LIVE FROM
THE OLYMPICS

Dad always told me it was better to be lucky than smart.
—Christine Brennan[1]

C HRISTINE'S FIRST Winter Olympics assignment for the *Post* was the Alpine skiing events in the Rocky Mountains west of Calgary. Alpine skiing involves the athletes racing down incredibly scary-looking, steep mountains at high rates of speed.

Christine learned a few lessons quickly during her first time covering the sport. Her press credentials also served as a lift pass for the mountain. Christine could ski anywhere to catch the action. Something else she picked up on in no time was that Olympic skiers are fast. *Very fast.* Olympic-level skiers fly down the mountain at an average of seventy-five to ninety-five miles an hour. All Christine could see while on the slope sidelines was a blur flying past her. She moved to the pressroom and watched the competition from the camera monitors. It was disappointing, because as her father would say, she couldn't "smell the action."

An unsuspecting hero of the Calgary skiing competitions was Michael "Eddie" Edwards, Britain's very first ski jumper. Eddie showed up with his thick, bottle-like glasses, borrowed ski boots, a helmet from the Italian team, and skis from the Austrians. The crowds watched as he stood at the top of the 70-meter jump. That's 230 feet high. Eddie adjusted his ski goggles, took a deep breath, and launched. With arms back behind him, and skis parallel, Eddie soared. He was somewhat awkward, and didn't make it too far down the slope, but he stayed upright. When he landed his jump, sports broadcasters announced, "The Eagle has landed!"

This phrase was first used on July 20, 1969, when Neil Armstrong announced to NASA's Mission Control in Houston that the Lunar Lander, named the Eagle, had successfully landed on the moon. Since then, the term is used to describe the completion of a mission.

Eddie came in dead last in the seventy- and ninety-meter jumps. But he said, "I was a true amateur and embodied what the Olympic spirit is all about."[2]

The United States athletes won very few medals in the Calgary Games. It had been fifty-two years since the country had won as few as they did in the Winter Olympics of 1988.[3] Although the United States team did not perform as well as a fan would hope for, as a journalist, Christine loved her first Winter Olympics experience.

There were many stories to cover, including the "Battle of the Brians." This was a term given to the intense competition between Brian Orser, a Canadian figure skater, and an American, Brian Boitano. Their competition is considered one of the most incredible in the history of men's figure skating. Brian Boitano ultimately won the gold medal, while Brian Orser won the silver.

Christine's next experience as a journalist covering the Olympics provided her with the opportunity to fly halfway around the world to the 1988 Summer Games in Seoul, South Korea.

Christine arrived jet-lagged, tired, and out of sorts; she felt that way for a week. Seoul's time was thirteen hours ahead of the *Post*'s offices

Christine in the press area, 1988 Olympics
Courtesy of Christine Brennan

in Washington, DC. If Christine was writing a story about an event that was happening at 6 p.m. on a Friday, it was 5 a.m. on Friday back in Washington. The time switch was so confusing some reporters wore two watches: one watch for the local time, the other for the time back home. It made watching the competitions and filing stories for deadline a challenge.

One evening Christine was supposed to go out with friends but decided to stop by the diving facility to catch some of the qualifying rounds of the three-meter springboard diving instead. She joked with her friends in the pressroom that she was going to watch "just in case someone hits their head."[4]

Christine ran into another reporter on the way to the diving complex and the two of them stumbled into one of the scariest moments in Olympic history. Christine sat just fifty feet away from American diver, Greg Louganis. She couldn't believe her luck. The two reporters watched as Greg climbed up the diving platform for his turn at qualifying. He strode confidently down the board. Greg thrust himself up off the board, reaching high with his muscular arms. Way up in the air, he grabbed his legs and began a triple reverse somersault. Once, twice, he spun perfectly through the air. Christine thought he looked too close to the board. He was. As he came out of the third rotation, the back of his head hit with a hard thud against the diving board. His body crumpled into the water. The crowd, many of them holding American flags, gasped.

Greg slowly surfaced to the water and swam to the side of the pool where his coach was waiting. He climbed up the pool ladder and held the back of his head. Christine and the many spectators sat, stunned at what they witnessed. "I think my pride was hurt more than anything else," he said.[5]

Amazingly, Greg got four temporary stitches and thirty minutes later was on the board again. He patted his heart before this dive, making the audience smile. Greg then prepared for a dive like the one he had just cracked his head on. Christine was nervous, holding her breath as he jumped. Greg executed the dive perfectly, and easily qualified for the competition. The next day, wearing a patch over his stitches, Greg battled with Tan Liangde of China throughout the ten-dive competition. It came down to the last dive. Greg performed the most difficult—a reverse three-and-one-half somersault—to perfection.

Christine's headline read, "Louganis Takes Gold After Hitting Board."[6]

"Whenever I'm asked about the heroic moments I remember most in sports, that's usually the one I mention first. Louganis went from that gruesome accident to winning the Olympic gold medal in twenty-four hours," Christine said.[7]

Ten days into the Olympics, Christine had the opportunity to share a big story from the Olympics. Unlike Greg Louganis's story though, this one didn't have a happy ending.

The story played out at the 100-meter event on the track in Seoul. The shortest distance in Olympic track and field competitions, 100

Christine and other members of the *Washington Post* staff, 1992 Olympics
Courtesy of Christine Brennan

meters is only 328 feet. Just like the alpine skiers whizzing down the slopes in Calgary, this race was so fast that the Canadian broadcasters barely began calling the race before it was over.

"*They are at the ready position. The gun, and it's a good clean start, and Ben Johnson gets a good start, and he is leading at this stage. Raymond Stewart trying to pick up, but, no, it is Ben Johnson leading. Ben Johnson has it. Ben Johnson has won an Olympic gold medal . . . Ben Johnson wins Olympic champion in a time of 9.79 seconds . . .*"[8]

Ben Johnson, a Jamaican-born sprinter living in Canada, took the gold in the one hundred meters in Seoul on September 24, 1988. The prime minister of Canada, Brian Mulroney, called immediately after the win to congratulate Ben personally.

Three days later, Christine's headline in the *Post* read "IOC Strips Johnson of Gold Medal in 100."

Ben Johnson's post-race drug test tested positive for a steroid, a drug that builds muscle. His gold medal was taken from him.

It was a heartbreaking ending for this athlete. Hailed as a hero in Canada after shattering the world record several years before, Ben had received sponsorship deals bringing in millions of dollars. He was considered a rock star in Europe and Japan. The world was at his feet. And then it was all gone, because of cheating. A sign in the Olympic Village read, "Hero to zero in 9.79 seconds."

Other athletes had tested positive for steroid and other drug use, but this was the first time that it occurred at the Olympics.

Christine had mixed emotions about covering the story. She hated how this scandal tarnished her beloved Olympics. But she also loved being in the thick of it. "We were on the cutting edge of one of the great issues of our day in sports," she said.[9]

The illegal use of steroids by athletes became one of the major topics of Christine's career from that point on.

Scandal was also at the heart of the biggest Olympic story that Christine has ever covered. Olympic champions don't just show up at the Games and compete. No matter what the sport, athletes practice, compete, and maintain rigid schedules, hoping to peak at the events held every four years.

Ice skating has become one of the Winter Olympics' premier sports. The beauty of the sport and its athletes, the costumes, and the technical aspects attract large audiences. The **subjective** awarding of points by individual judges draws viewers in, while also confusing them.

In 1986 the International Olympic Committee voted to have the Summer and Winter Games held in separate years. So currently, even though the Olympics are four years apart, the Summer and Winter Olympics are always two years apart. To adjust the schedule, the 1994 Winter Olympics were held in Lillehammer, Norway, only two years after the 1992 Games in Albertville, France. It was the first and only time two Winter Olympics were held just two years apart, so the rivalry between winter athletes was even more intense than usual.

This stiff competition was behind one of the most bizarre incidents in Olympic history.

The US Olympic figure skating trials were taking place at the Joe Louis Arena in Detroit, Michigan, in early January 1994. On the ice at different times were the two rivals: Tonya Harding and Nancy Kerrigan. The competition was tough, as only two skaters from a field of twenty would be chosen to go to the Olympics.

Tonya was raised in Portland, Oregon. She was greatly influenced by her demanding, abusive, alcoholic mother. The family was poor, as her father, a truck driver, often couldn't work because of health problems. They couldn't afford private ice time. Tonya grew up practicing at a skating rink inside a nearby mall, where she trained herself to become a tough, competitive athlete. Tonya's athleticism and determination spoke for themselves. She was the first female skater in the United States to successfully nail a triple axel, a jump involving three revolutions, or spins, in the air, in competition, several years before at the 1991 United States Championships. But she showed up late for the 1992 Olympics and didn't look like she was prepared for competition. Tonya placed fourth. She vowed to make a comeback in 1994. Yet, outside distractions, including marrying an abusive man, didn't help her efforts.

Nancy grew up in Massachusetts. She, too, came from a blue-collar background. Her father was a welder, often working two jobs to feed the family of five. Nancy's mother was legally blind and ran the household. Christine said Nancy "was a feisty, Boston tomboy who would play hockey with her brothers."[10]

Although she was a tomboy, Nancy looked the part of a model figure skater and was incredibly graceful on the ice. Nancy also competed at the 1992 Olympics, nudging Tonya out of a medal by taking the bronze medal. She had her sights on gold for the 1994 Olympics.

Nancy had just finished her practice session in Detroit and skated off the ice. She stopped to put her skate guards on. She walked in front of her coaches toward a curtain covering up the entryway to a hall leading back to the dressing rooms. Her coaches stopped to talk to friends. Soon after, they heard screams coming from behind the curtain that Nancy just walked through.

Christine, rinkside at the 1994 Winter Olympics

Courtesy of Christine Brennan

Christine was there, covering the Olympic trials. She, along with several other writers assigned to the Olympic beat, was watching the pairs short program when she heard that a skater had been injured. Christine and the other journalists went to the pressroom to discover more details.

A man had apparently come out of nowhere with a collapsible metal pipe in his hand and hit Nancy on the knee with the pipe. Hard.

Her coaches found her on the strip of carpet leading back to the dressing rooms, screaming and crying, "Why me, why, why?"[11]

Why indeed. Why would someone want to injure her? And what would happen with only five weeks until the Olympics?

Ultimately it was determined that Tonya's ex-husband had hired several men to carry out the attack to make sure that Tonya made the team. Tonya maintained her innocence.

The injury to Nancy's knee was a severe bone bruise. She went through intense physical therapy to prepare herself for the Olympics, in which she hoped to compete. The International Olympic Committee chose both Tonya and Nancy to compete.

The world watched as Tonya's Olympic performance literally unraveled due to a broken skating lace during her long program. Nancy skated perfectly, narrowly missing out on the gold medal. Nancy brought home the silver.

Tonya came home to face the fall-out of the assault of Nancy Kerrigan. Tonya admitted to being aware of her husband's actions after the incident and not sharing this with investigators at the time. The United States Figure Skating Association stripped Tonya of her 1994 US Championships title. More significantly, she was banned from the USFSA for life. Tonya Harding could never skate competitively or professionally again.

Nancy Kerrigan was heralded as the champion she was and received millions in sponsorship deals.[12]

As the drama unfolded over the course of seven weeks, it provided Christine with plenty of material for her articles with the *Post*.

THE COST OF BECOMING
A FIGURE SKATING OLYMPIAN

THOSE WITH DREAMS of making it to the Olympics as a figure skater need talent, a strong work ethic, and time. Future
Olympians train for up to three hours a day as soon as they can
lace up their skates. A figure skater also needs money for all the
expenses involved—lots of money. It is estimated that between
private ice time, coaching, costumes, skates, and travel expenses, it costs about $100,000 per year to train and compete
at that level.[13]

Christine became well informed on the whole situation. She flew
from coast to coast covering the story. She went to Boston to cover
Nancy's first practice after the attack. Then she flew to Portland to report on Tonya. While out in Oregon, Christine met Sara Just, who was
the producer of the ABC News show, *Nightline*. Sara was looking for a
source to speak about the aftermath of the attack on the show. Christine made her debut on *Nightline* a week later.

After that coverage, Christine became the source for all things re-
lated to Tonya and Nancy. She was featured on CNN, ESPN, and NPR.
Viewers of the ABC and NBC evening news saw Christine reporting.
Meet the Press and the *Today* show came calling. And Christine responded. Her family back home was seeing her on the television more
than they were in person. Her brother Jim told his mom he was tired
of seeing Christine on television so much.

The story became so big that it provided new opportunities for
Christine.

DID YOU KNOW?

Fashion designer Vera Wang has created costumes for many well-known figure skating champions, including Evan Lysacek, Nancy Kerrigan, and Michelle Kwan. When she was a child, Vera dreamed of competing in the Olympics as a skater. She even competed in the US Nationals in 1968. However, she did not make the team, so Vera hung up her ice skates.

EIGHT

FIGURE SKATING

Figure skating is the best sport.
—Michael Janofsky, *New York Times* reporter[1]

C HRISTINE'S LOVE for figure skating began long before her reporting on the Winter Olympics, on a small patch of ice her dad put on the back patio. Her siblings were much better at navigating the ice on their blades. However, the sounds, *swish-swish*, and feeling of floating on ice ignited a passion for the sport Christine still feels today.

Christine found a heroine on the ice in Dorothy Hamill during the 1976 Olympics. Dorothy was a nineteen-year-old from Connecticut who had won several US Championships. Dorothy created a new move, called the Hamill camel, where she took a camel spin, a maneuver with the skater bent at the waist and one leg extended out, into a sit spin.

The 1976 Winter Olympics were in Innsbruck, Austria. Christine couldn't wait to learn how Dorothy performed at the Olympics. Christine figured out that Toledo was six time zones behind Austria. It was nighttime in Austria, but afternoon in Toledo. Christine listened to the

Toledo all-news radio station broadcasting the figure skating performances live. She listened to the reports from her bedroom as the announcement came on that Dorothy was about to skate her long program. The music played; Christine could hear the cheers of the audience throughout the performance. And then came the announcement. Dorothy Hamill won the gold medal. Christine jumped up and down on her bed, thrilled.

Christine began reporting on the sport for the *Post* in 1988 and is now considered an expert in the field.

When she began sharing stories about the skaters and their performances, Christine drew upon the lesson she learned so many years before while listening to the radio play-by-play calls of her beloved Toledo Mud Hens. The announcer wasn't describing the players or their uniforms. It was hard for young Christine to imagine what the players looked like, or even know who they were while listening to the broadcasts. Reporting on ice skating was a dream for this journalist. Christine learned to share all aspects of the competitions she was reporting on so that her audiences felt like they were *there*.

From the cold feel of the ice arenas to the judges' reactions to the music selections and the beautiful costumes, Christine covered it all.

Christine's expertise in figure skating took her in directions that she had only dreamed of. First, she was offered a job with ESPN to be an on-air reporter at its Chicago bureau. It was a wonderful opportunity. Christine struggled with whether to take the job. Her family helped her make the decision. They felt that Christine would not be as happy at ESPN as she was covering the Olympics for the *Post*. Christine decided to stay at the *Post*.

Then another opportunity became a reality. Due to her exposure and involvement with skaters through her reporting, Christine wanted to write a book about the sport. There were very few books on the subject at the time. Christine proposed the idea to an editor with Scribner publishing house. They accepted the proposal. They were going to publish Christine's book on figure skating.

Greetings from White Ring Arena
1998 Winter Olympics
Nagano, Japan

Christine displays her second book on figure skating, *Edge of Glory,* from the White Ring Arena, 1998 Winter Olympics, Nagano, Japan.

Christine and Scott Hamilton announce the US Figure Skating Championships, Kansas City, 2017.

Courtesy of Christine Brennan

Christine was allowed to step away from her job at the *Post*—an eight-month leave—to write her book. During that time frame, Christine followed many skaters throughout the 1994–95 season. *Inside Edge* became a bestseller when it debuted at the same time as the US Figure Skating Championships in 1996.

In *Inside Edge*, Christine revealed the challenges those who are new to the sport face. Christine shared Jenni Tew's story. Jenni's mother moved with Jenni and her younger sister to be closer to a coach in the Cleveland area. Her father commuted from Florida every other weekend. For all her time and effort, Jenni's best finish was fifth in the junior level competition at the 1997 US Figure Skating Championships.

Christine also wrote about more seasoned skaters, including Scott Hamilton. Scott is also from Northwest Ohio. Born in Toledo, he was adopted by a couple who lived in Bowling Green, Ohio.

Skater Brian Boitano takes a selfie photograph at the 2016 US Figure Skating Championships that includes Christine and (*left to right*) Dorothy Hamill, Tom Collins, the longtime owner of the Champions on Ice skating tour, and Michelle Kwan.

Courtesy of Christine Brennan

Scott was a fireball of energy on the ice. Scott is small—five feet three inches tall—and he weighed just over one hundred pounds at the height of his amateur skating days. As a child, he suffered from a mysterious illness that kept his body from digesting food. He started skating at the age of four, which likely helped cure the illness four years later, but his growth was limited.

Scott took full advantage of his compact frame, barreling around the ice and dropping his signature back flips as never seen before. He won four consecutive World Championships, and four consecutive US Figure Skating Championships. Scott's performance at the 1984 Winter Olympics in Sarajevo earned him the gold medal.

Scott performed in many ice shows after turning professional, including one that Christine wrote about in *Inside Edge*. Scott, now a father of four, including two children he and his wife, Tracie, adopted from Haiti, is also a cancer survivor. Scott established the Scott Hamilton CARES Foundation, which supports cancer research and cancer patients. He still finds time to cover the sport, as he did with Christine at the 2017 US Figure Skating Championships in Kansas City, Missouri.

Christine also wrote about skaters who were in the thick of their career, including Michael Weiss. At the time, Michael was coming off a disastrous performance at the US Nationals in 1995. He fell twice at the start of his performance. Michael managed to get up both times, dust himself off, and do the best he could do to recover. But the damage was done.

Michael continued to compete, however, and went on to win three national titles in 1999, 2000, and 2003; two world bronze medals in 1999 and 2000; and to compete in the Olympics in 1998 and 2002.

Michael gave back to the sport that gave him so much. He organized skating shows with the concept of "skaters helping skaters." Through the show, Michael, his wife, Lisa, and his mother, Margie, raised hundreds of thousands of dollars for scholarships to help skaters with training costs. In 2011, the emcee of his show was none other than Christine.

Christine continued to cover figure skating and the Olympics for the *Washington Post* through 1996. She left the newspaper after the Games that year. As she explained, she didn't leave because there was anything wrong. *Just the opposite.* Everything was going right for Christine. She was offered a contract to write another book on figure skating. She also signed on with CBS Sports to report on several figure skating stories. Christine signed on with a national speakers' bureau and continued doing work for National Public Radio's *Morning Edition.* Christine felt excited about the opportunities and whatever might come next.

What came next would give Christine a bigger platform then she ever expected.

IT'S ALL IN THE JUMPING!

FIGURE SKATERS make jumps look simple. Yet, each jump consists of technical requirements that are very difficult.

The six most common jumps in competitive figure skating can be divided into two categories: toe jumps and edge jumps. Toe jumps include the toe loop, flip, and Lutz. The edge jumps are the Salchow, loop, and Axel. The main difference between the two categories is that in the toe jumps, skaters use the toe-pick of their free leg to help propel them into the air. The skater kicks the front of the ice skating blade—the toe—into the ice to start a toe jump.[2]

Tonya Harding was the first woman to land two triple axels in competition in 1991. Kurt Browning was the first man to land a quadruple jump—in his case, a quadruple loop—in competition in 1988.

DID YOU KNOW?

Seventeen-year-old Nathan Chen was the first skater to successfully land five quadruple jumps during competition at the US Figure Skating Championships in 2017.

NINE

GOING NATIONAL

. . . one friend jokingly nicknamed me "Crusades and Hand Grenades."'

—Christine Brennan[1]

U*SA TODAY* has a daily readership of nearly three million people.[2] It's the largest circulation newspaper in the United States. Since August 1997, those millions of readers have had the opportunity to witness Christine's take on the world of sports and the world with sports in it.

It all began when Christine had lunch with *USA Today* sports editor, Monte Lorell. He asked her to come onboard as a columnist for the sports section. Christine accepted his offer. She's been with the paper ever since.

In what was a natural transition from her role with the *Washington Post*, Christine began writing about figure skating for a special Olympic section being published by *USA Today*. The upcoming Winter Olympics were being held in Nagano, Japan, in February 1998. The paper sent her to Japan to cover the Olympics. While she was there,

USA Today ran this head shot of Christine on her column.

Courtesy of Christine Brennan

Christine wrote daily stories for the paper, and completed the final chapters on her newest book *Edge of Glory*.

Never one to be still, Christine also served as an analyst on figure skating for both ABC News and ESPN. She was one busy lady!

She didn't want it any other way. She loves what she does. "I've never worked a day in my life. I am doing what I love, and for the young people out there, boys and girls, men and women, whatever, who are thinking about life and what they'd like to do, if you do what you love, you never work a day in your life," Christine said.[3]

Christine's role with *USA Today* has provided her with the opportunity to not only cover a variety of sports around the world, but to shed light on wrongdoing, discrimination issues, and other injustices in the arena of sports. Just as Christine's audience grew, so too did her voice. And she's not afraid to use it.

Christine on the air with Trey Wingo at the ESPN Sports Center during the 2002 Winter Olympics in Salt Lake City

Courtesy of Christine Brennan

One of the first opportunities to use that voice involved Augusta National Golf Club, the very private golf course in Georgia that hosts the annual prestigious Masters Tournament. Christine had never been sent by the *Post* to cover any golf events, much less one that is considered the ultimate tournament. For sportswriters, covering the Masters is the "plum assignment of the year."[4]

The golf course at Augusta is so pristine one is almost hesitant to walk on it. The **rough**, the grass that is usually longer and "rougher", is nicer than most golf courses' **fairways**. The grounds crew works endless hours to ensure that the azaleas surrounding many holes are at the peak of their bloom the week of the Masters every year.

Christine mentioned to friends that she had never been to the course before when she arrived at the media center at the clubhouse. A fellow reporter took her to an area on the course called Amen Corner. This section of the golf course is where the eleventh, twelfth, and thirteenth golf holes come together. It receives the most attention during the television coverage of the tournament. Christine observed the beautiful flowers, gorgeous golf holes, and quiet atmosphere. She also noticed that most of the fans attending the event were white, and the staff who were picking up trash were black.

Augusta National Golf Club is one of the most private golf facilities in the United States. *In the world.* The golf course is off limits to play from mid-May to mid-October in fear that the combination of heat and play would damage the turf. Summer and fall are when golf is played. So why would someone want to pay the estimated $25,000 to $50,000 to join and another $10,000 a year for such a limited time frame? The answer is simple: Prestige. Status. Membership is by invitation only, and there are just three hundred members who belong to the club.

When Christine visited for that first time in 1999, she wondered if the club had any black or female members. So, she asked during the press conference being held by the new chairman of the club, Hootie Johnson. After a few other reporters had asked their questions, Christine raised her hand. She asked how many African American members and how many female members there were at the club.

Johnson replied, "Well, that's a club matter, and all club matters are private."

Christine persisted, as any good journalist would. "Are there women members?"

Johnson's response was the same: It was a private matter.[5]

Christine's column in the April 11, 1999, issue of *USA Today* began with, "I made a right turn off the main drag in Augusta the other day and ended up in 1975. Or perhaps it was 1940. It was hard to tell."[6]

The truth was the Augusta National Golf Club admitted its first African American member in 1990. It wouldn't be until 2012 that the club's first female members were admitted. Christine's direct question

Christine in front of the "Bird's Nest" at the 2008 Summer Olympics, Beijing
Courtesy of Christine Brennan

was at the heart of the change. A column that she wrote three years after her visit to Augusta in April 2002, about the lack of female members at the club, caught the eye of a woman who just happened to pick up a copy of the newspaper. That woman was Martha Burk, who was the Chair of the National Council of Women's Organizations, which represents over eleven million women.

It took ten years, but finally, through the efforts of many women and men, both former Secretary of State Condoleezza Rice and businesswoman Darla Moore were admitted as members to the private club. Christine got the scoop and broke the news. The headline of Christine's column on August 20, 2012, read, "Finally! Augusta National does right thing and admits women."

Christine wrote, "It's not really about allowing women to belong and play golf at an exclusive, beautiful, private club. It's about letting them participate in the process that continues to build our nation."[7]

MAKING HISTORY AT AUGUSTA NATIONAL GOLF CLUB

CONDOLEEZZA RICE and Darla Moore are known as the first two female members of Augusta National Golf Club.

Condoleezza was born in segregated Alabama in 1954. She moved with her parents, both teachers, to Denver, Colorado, while Condoleezza was in high school. She graduated from the University of Denver with a degree in political science and a passion for playing the piano. Condoleezza obtained a master's degree a year later from Notre Dame, and a doctorate in Russian Studies from the University of Denver. She went on to teach at Stanford University in California. Washington, DC, lured her away from academic life beginning in the mid-1980s. She served on the Joint Chiefs of Staff, as director of Soviet and East European affairs with the National Security Council, and as special assistant to President H. W. Bush during the dissolution, or breaking up, of the Soviet Union. In 2001 she became the first black woman appointed to the post of National Security Advisor under President George W. Bush. She became the sixty-sixth secretary of state for the United States in 2004. Condoleezza has returned to her beloved Stanford University, where she became the first woman provost in 1993.

Darla grew up in Lake City, South Carolina, on a farm that grew cotton, soybeans, and tobacco. She obtained her bachelor's degree in political science in just three years from the University of South Carolina and obtained her Master of Business Administration (MBA) from George Washington University. Darla worked for Chemical Bank, and then became vice president of a private investment company, Rainwater, Inc. Darla has given millions of dollars to her undergraduate **alma mater**, where the business school is named after her. She is founder of the Palmetto Institute, an organization that strives to increase the income of South Carolina residents. Darla has the distinction of being the first woman profiled on the cover of *Fortune* magazine.

Christine reporting from the 2014 Winter Olympics, Sochi, Russia
Courtesy of Christine Brennan

Christine continues to shed light on issues within the world of sports in her stories for *USA Today*. She's written about the Russian judging scandal in the figure skating competition at the 2014 Olympic Games in Sochi. One of the judges was married to the general manager of the Russian skating organization. Another judge had been punished years before for trying to "fix" the 1998 Winter Olympics. **Allegations** of unfair judging in the sport of figure skating has been an issue for a long time.

Christine is trying to use her voice to make things fairer for all skaters.

American Ashley Wagner placed seventh in the 2014 Olympics, despite not falling in either her short or long program. A Russian skater placed fifth even though she fell in both programs. "This sport needs to be held more accountable with its system if they want people to believe in it," Ashley said after the competition.[8]

Christine has called for National Football League owners to stop hiring and defending players who physically abuse women. "Every time an NFL player punches his wife or girlfriend, the list of the league's alarmingly out-of-touch owners grows longer," Christine wrote in her *USA Today* column on October 26, 2016.[9]

The National Football League created a new policy in 2014 to try to end the acceptance of acts of violence off the field by players. It hasn't made much of a difference. Christine wrote in her column in *USA Today* that the NFL owners should be looked upon as leaders. But in this important matter, she wrote, they aren't. "They are followers, refusing to take any kind of a moral stand, bowing to their team's needs on the field at every turn, unable to muster the least bit of outrage, finally changing their stance only when the rest of the world crashes in on them."[10]

Owners of the National Football League teams are still hiring football players with known domestic violence records. Christine asked, "Do these owners ever learn? Do they want to?"[11]

Christine also believes that Olympic athletes should be held to a higher standard. They should never cheat or lie. American swimmer Ryan Lochte lied at the 2016 Olympic Games in Rio de Janeiro and ultimately cheated his peers out of their moment in the spotlight.

Ryan Lochte has won twelve Olympic gold medals, including one in a relay at the 2016 Games. After he was through competing, he went out celebrating with three other American swimmers. When Ryan and the other swimmers returned to the Olympic Village, he claimed that they had been robbed at gunpoint by men with police badges. But Ryan made up the story. What really happened is Ryan and his teammates destroyed property and were caught.

As the true details of the night became public, Christine and her fellow journalists, along with the rest of the world, were outraged. Christine called for Ryan Lochte to apologize to the city of Rio. She also wrote that he should apologize to the Olympic Committee, athletes,

Christine at the 2016 Summer Olympic Games, Rio de Janeiro, Brazil
Courtesy of Christine Brennan

and anyone associated, as his actions took the focus away from where it should be. "Shame on him," she wrote.[12]

Ryan Lochte was suspended for ten months and not allowed to participate in the 2017 World Championships as a result of his actions.

Christine was on top of the story from the beginning.

"I was able to break so much of that story because I'm a veteran and know all the people making the decisions. Just being able to call or text contacts to get the story . . . is a result of years of wonderful working relationships with people. Then they call you and you get the scoop. It is journalism in its best form, relationships, decades in the making. It's all about treating people right, and they'll treat you right. It's important to never reveal names, to keep quiet about sources. If you've got the confidence, and the goods, you've got the story."[13]

Christine says breaking a story is the greatest feeling in the world.

Whenever Christine sees injustice in the world of sports, she uses her strong voice and leadership role to try to make a difference. Whether reporting on an Olympic athlete caught lying and cheating, sexist comments about female athletes made by her peers, or unacceptable behavior by an athlete or coach, Christine is there, covering the story and offering her opinions.

"I feel there is a lot of right and wrong in this world. I feel that there is a lot of gray area but also a lot of black and white, and when an athlete misbehaves or when something bad happens in sports, I will happily bring that up. I don't care if I get hundreds of emails that **despise** what I said or did. It probably means I'm doing the right thing."[14]

USA Today has created ads featuring Christine. They read, "You can count on her to tell it like it is." She certainly does.

"I want people to be angry with me. That means I'm doing my job," Christine said.[15]

Christine has received lots of letters, e-mails, and communication through social media because of her strong voice over the years. "The nastiness used to come in the form of letters when I was covering the NFL beat for the *Washington Post* in the mid-to-late 1980s," Christine said. They wrote things like "Go back to the kitchen where you belong" to her.[16]

Christine is not alone. Many female sports journalists suffer from indirect, mean communications on social media. But, as Christine shared, those who choose to post such ugly comments will not deter female sports journalists. In fact, those comments may encourage them.

"There are more than one thousand of us working in sports media in the United States, with hundreds more wanting to get into the business annually. This year, 145 female college students applied for the eight scholarships being offered by the Association for Women in Sports Media," she wrote. "Next year there will be another 145 or more. A few angry people on social media won't stop any of them."[17]

And, Christine is doing everything she can to support, mentor, and encourage her successors, those who follow in her footsteps in the field.

Christine displays *USA Today*'s promotional ad for her column while seated in the Rose Bowl Press Room, 2015.

Courtesy of Christine Brennan

DID YOU KNOW?

Augusta National Golf Club also named IBM Chief Executive Officer Virginia (Ginny) Rometty as the third female member in 2014.

TEN

PASSING THE BATON

I hope I have helped. I hope some little girl out there knows now that she can be a sportswriter if she wants to be.

—Mary Garber[1]

The BEST SEAT in the house is considered *the* place to be for any sporting event. From the best seat in the house one can see the sweat of the athletes and feel the tension of the competitors. One can hear the slice of the skating blade on the ice or the groans of the football players while on the field.

Christine used this phrase as the title of her memoir, published in 2006. In her story, Christine reflects on her relationship with her father, Jim, her life playing and reporting on sports, and her personal life.

Christine's father was a great influence on her throughout her life, encouraging her to play sports when not many other girls did and to play them properly. Jim challenged her to get good grades and to be the best that she could at whatever she attempted. Her father championed her through the tough times and offered advice during difficult times in her career.

Christine signing copies of her memoir, *Best Seat In The House*
Courtesy of Christine Brennan

Christine's parents' loving marriage and her wonderful childhood with her siblings gave her a strong foundation. Although Christine's path in life didn't allow for a similar lifestyle, Christine is blessed with a wealth of friends and family members along with her amazing career. Christine has never married, although she came close twice (two men in the world of sports journalism). She doesn't have children of her own to pass her lessons on to, but that hasn't stopped her from sharing with young people. First and foremost, she has a wonderful relationship with her nieces and nephews. Christine has made it a point to go back to Toledo often, witnessing the various school activities of her siblings' children. And, now that some of them are older and on their own, they visit Christine in Washington.

Christine also passes her hard-earned lessons on to future journalists.

Christine and her dad, Jim
Courtesy of Christine Brennan

Although Christine continues to occupy the best seat in the house, she is also mentoring younger people who want to be like her, to sit in her seat.

Christine is still reporting on sports for *USA Today* as well as continuing in various other roles. Whether she is in the press box at the Super Bowl, rinkside at the US Figure Skating Championships, or traveling around the globe chasing down stories at the Olympics, Christine holds court in her role as sports journalist and commentator.

Equally important, Christine is keeping the seat warm for those who are studying and working toward sliding into the chair beside her. Christine is a shining example of taking one's passions, putting them to use in the world, and then encouraging others to follow in her footsteps.

These days Christine can often be found in lecture halls, sharing her wisdom with journalism students. Speaking at a lectern, with one of her favorite scarves from an artist in Toledo wrapped around her neck, honoring the wisdom from her father, Christine stands up straight and looks people in the eye, sharing her insights with students entering the field.

Her advice, based on many years of experience, runs from making sure to "double check and triple check" the facts to writing thank-you notes—actual thank-you notes, the kind that you hand write on a notecard, put in an envelope, and stick a stamp on. "You'll knock the socks off of anyone you've interviewed with if you send them a thank-you note,"[2] she said.

Watching sports is meant to be entertaining. It is no longer all fun and games though. Christine admits that it is a different world today than it was when she started reporting. "We look to sports to take us to other places, to escape, but increasingly, it is no longer an escape with these issues, but much more a reflection on our society," she said.[3]

It is also a different world from the days when she would interview athletes in a locker room, race to the press room with her laptop, and knock out the story in no time flat to make deadline. Now stories are broadcast almost even as the events are still happening. But one thing hasn't changed. As she tells students: "Make sure to get the story right. I worry that this push to get everything done so quickly leaves too much room for mistakes and sloppiness. We all need to take a few extra minutes to double-check everything. You're only as good as your last story, and reputations and careers can be lost in a second if you don't live by the wonderful journalistic ethics you're being taught in school."[4]

Being right and getting the story right are sometimes two different things, Christine feels. She encourages students to express opinion only based on fact. To do otherwise is simply wrong. "Nothing is more important than your reputation," Christine offered.[5] Christine also cautions students to be okay with holding back on breaking a story until facts are gathered and to tell an editor that they don't quite have the story right yet.

Mentoring students, especially young women interested in sports journalism as their career, is a passion for Christine. On her website,

Christine, with her parents, Jim and Betty, at the ceremony inducting her into the Ohio Women's Hall of Fame in Columbus, Ohio

Courtesy of Christine Brennan

right along with tabs offering information on her books and her writing, is a tab titled "Students." In large letters is one of her biggest nuggets of wisdom: INTERNSHIPS ARE EVERYTHING. As she learned during her college years while working at the *Blade* in Toledo and the *Herald* in Miami, internships helped open doors to her as a sports journalist. Northwestern's Medill School of Journalism is recognized as being one of the leaders in the field in providing students with hands-on experience in internships.

Young female sports journalists also have something that Christine had very little of during her early years—peers. When Christine began her career, she was one of just a handful of female writers reporting on the sidelines, in the locker rooms, and at the training camps. Now there are over a thousand women sportswriters.

A huge part of this growth comes from an organization established in 1987. The Association for Women in Sports Media (AWSM) was created to promote internships and diversity in sports media. Christine

Christine with AWSM founder, Kristin Huckshorn
Arianna Grainey/AWSM, photographer

was the first president of the organization. And, based on a suggestion from her sister Kate, Christine has established scholarships awarded by the organization in honor of her parents. The Jim Brennan and Betty Brennan scholarships are awarded annually in memory of her beloved parents. Betty died in 2002, and Jim just a year later.

In addition to the scholarships Christine has established, AWSM offers several other annual scholarships. Since the beginning of the scholarship program in 1990, AWSM has arranged for paid summer internships for over 140 female college students interested in sports media careers. Internships range from broadcast production, broadcast reporting, print/digital reporting, to magazine writing and public relations. Every intern receives a $1,000 scholarship and complimentary registration and lodging at AWSM's annual convention.

Along with continually giving her time to future sports journalists, Christine also dedicates a lot of time to her hometown of Toledo and her alma mater, Northwestern. She still owns the family home in Ottawa Hills and returns for visits with her siblings and their families.

Christine with AWSM scholarship winners: (*left to right*) Hannah Burton and Callie Caplan, 2016

Arianna Grainey/AWSM, photographer

Christine often appears at benefits and gave the 2008 winter commencement speech at the University of Toledo. The University of Toledo bestowed an honorary degree on her that day, one of two she has earned thus far for her accomplishments in her field and her role as mentor and trailblazer.

The theme of her speech? In the immortal words of her father, "This ain't no dress rehearsal."[6]

Christine was invited back to the University of Toledo to serve as the speaker for the 2017 spring graduates. She talked about her passion for sports, which started right there, in the University of Toledo Glass Bowl stadium watching the Rockets' undefeated seasons from 1969 through 1971. She spoke of the lessons she learned from her father, as he shared stories during timeouts and at halftime. He had told Christine and her siblings that nothing comes easy, success is up to you, listen before you speak, show respect and kindness to others, be positive, act like you belong in the room, and live life to the fullest.

MARY GARBER, THE FIRST
WOMAN SPORTSWRITER

MARY GREW UP much like Christine did: playing sports and writing. She, too, created her own newsletter, the *Garber News*. After graduating from Hollins College in Roanoke, Virginia, Mary took a job as a society writer, covering fancy events for the *Twin City Sentinel*, a newspaper in Winston-Salem, North Carolina. It was not Mary's ideal job in journalism. At one dance, Mary shared, "I got the wrong dress on the wrong lady."[7]

Mary began filling in for the sports department at the newspaper during World War II. She eventually worked full-time as a sportswriter for the *Sentinel* and then for the *Winston-Salem Journal*. Tiny Mary—just five feet tall, weighing less than one hundred pounds—was a big presence in her trademark knit cap, taking notes on the sidelines.

Mary was not only the first female sportswriter, she also broke barriers by covering sports at African American high schools and colleges. As a result of her hard work and determination, Mary was the first woman to receive the Associated Press Sports Editors Red Smith Award in 2005. This award has been given every year for major contributions to sports journalism. Mary was ninety-two years old when she died in 2008.

Journalist Mary Garber

Courtesy of Forsyth County Public Library Photograph Collection, Winston-Salem, NC

The high standards that her parents expected of Christine are the same ones she expects of others. Her thrill over breaking a story and sharing with readers will never go away, nor will her enthusiasm for teaching and mentoring young people.

Christine is an inspiration not only to up-and-coming students, but also—in at least one instance—to an athlete as well. While writing her book, *Inside Edge*, Christine had the opportunity to meet with Janet Lynn, one of the greatest figure skaters of all time.

After her skating career was over, Janet lived a quiet life out of the spotlight, raising five young sons near Detroit, Michigan. Christine wasn't sure that Janet would meet with her for an interview. At the most, she thought, Janet might give her five minutes of her time. Instead, after she and Janet talked for four-and-a-half hours, Christine had to excuse herself from the interview due to a previous commitment. Dorothy Hamill had always been her favorite skater; now Christine had a new favorite, that mother of five, former world champion Janet Lynn.

Christine would often call Janet while working on *Inside Edge*, telling her that many of the other skaters would say that Janet was their favorite too. Janet couldn't believe it. Christine sent her one of her author's copies of *Inside Edge*. After she read the book, Janet called Christine to share a secret.

She was back on the ice, skating. Every so often she'd get up early in the morning before her family was up and go to the Detroit Skating Club and glide around the ice. She had Christine to thank for getting her back out there.[8]

Christine's father and mentors taught Christine many lessons: practice makes perfect; always do something properly; it is important to give of oneself and to encourage others; and find whatever your passion is and to dedicate yourself to it.

She continues to practice what she learned in her roles as *USA Today* columnist, commentator, author, and professional speaker.

She continues to pass those lessons on to all of us.

Christine with Frank Sesno at the CNN Washington bureau desk
Courtesy of Christine Brennan

DID YOU KNOW?

The Association for Women in Sports Media (AWSM) presents an award in honor of Mary Garber annually to a woman in the industry who has served as a role model. Christine Brennan was the 2004 recipient of the Mary Garber Pioneer Award.

Christine's Timeline

May 14, 1958

Christine Brennan is born in Toledo to Jim and Betty Brennan

Fall 1976

Christine starts attending classes at Northwestern Medill School of Journalism

Summer 1978

Christine works as an intern at the *Toledo Blade* in Toledo, Ohio

Summer 1979

Christine works as an intern in the sports department of the *Toledo Blade*

Spring 1980

Christine graduates from Northwestern University

Summer 1980

Christine interns at the *Miami Herald*

Spring 1981

Christine obtains a master's degree in journalism from Northwestern

Summer 1981

Christine begins career at the *Miami Herald*

1984

Christine's first book, *The Miracle of Miami,* is published

July–August 1984

Christine covers her first Olympics Games in Los Angeles for the *Miami Herald*

September 1984

Christine is hired by the *Washington Post* as the first female to cover the National Football League's Washington, DC, team

1988

Christine is elected as the first president of the Association for Women in Sports Media (AWSM)

January 1996

Christine's book *Inside Edge* is released

August 1997

Christine begins writing a weekly column for *USA Today*

1999

Christine signs a contract with ABC News

Christine reports on the lack of female members at Augusta National Golf Club

2006

Christine's memoir, *Best Seat in the House,* is released

September 2013

Christine is elected to serve on Northwestern University's Board of Trustees

Christine's Awards and Recognitions

1993
   Capital Press Women's "Woman of Achievement"

1995
   Inductee—Ohio Women's Hall of Fame

2001 & 2003
   Associated Press Sports Editors—Top ten columnists in the category of the nation's biggest newspapers

2002
   University of North Carolina's Reed Sarratt Distinguished Lecturer
   US Sports Academy's Ronald Reagan Media Award

2003
   Jake Wade Award from the College Sports Information Directors of America for outstanding media contribution to intercollegiate athletics

2004
   Association for Women in Sports Media—Pioneer Award
   Northwestern University Medill School of Journalism Hall of Achievement inductee

2005
   Woman of the Year from WISE (Women in Sports and Events)

2006
   Inaugural Women's Sports Foundation Billie Award in Journalism
   Chi Omega's Woman of Achievement Award
   Inductee—Ottawa Hills (Ohio) Foundation Hall of Fame
   Alumnae Award winner from The Alumnae of Northwestern University

2007
   Northwestern University's Alumni Service Award

2008

Inaugural Northwestern University Women's Athletics Alumnae Award

2013

Yale University's Kiphuth Medal

Ralph McGill Lecturer at the University of Georgia.

2017

Northwestern University Athletic Hall of Fame (Honorary)

Glossary

allegation: a claim that someone has done something illegal or wrong

alma mater: college or university from which an individual has graduated

apartheid: in South Africa, a policy of segregation or discrimination on grounds of race

base: in geometry, a line on which a figure is considered standing: the base of the triangle

beat: a reporter's routine covering of the same news sources

Big Ten: the oldest Division I collegiate athletic conference in the United States, established in 1895. As of 2018, the fourteen member schools of the Big Ten, all predominantly major research universities with strong academic reputations, are Indiana University, Michigan State University, Northwestern University, Ohio State University, Pennsylvania State University, Purdue University, Rutgers University-New Brunswick, University of Illinois, University of Iowa, University of Maryland, University of Michigan, University of Minnesota, University of Nebraska, and the University of Wisconsin.

boycott: refuse to cooperate or participate in

bureau: office or department for doing specific business

byline: in a newspaper, the line naming the writer of a story

city desk: the department of a newspaper dealing with local news

clippings: articles cut from a magazine or newspaper

credentials: a document proving one's identity or qualifications

deadline: the latest date by which something should be completed

despise: feel contempt or a deep dislike for

expatriate: a person who lives outside his or her native country

exponents: in mathematics, a quantity representing the power to which a given number is to be raised, usually represented as a raised numeral beside the number

fairway: the mowed part of any hole of a golf course between the tee (where the golfer hits, or drives, the first ball) and the green (where play is completed by gently hitting, or putting, the ball into the golf hole)

feminism: the belief in, and promotion of, women's rights on the grounds of political, social, and economic equality to men

forte: something one excels at

Maccabiah Games: first held in 1932, an international Jewish sport competition held once every four years in Israel

mentor: to advise and train; an experienced person who counsels and trains new employees or students

morbid: appealing to an unhealthy interest in unpleasant subjects such as death

powers: in mathematics, the product obtained when a number is multiplied by itself a certain number of times. For example: two to the power of four equals sixteen.

previews: commentary on a forthcoming book or film

red-shirt: a college athlete who is withdrawn from participating in sporting contests for a year in order to develop skills and extend playing eligibility for an additional year

roster: a list of members of a team or organization

rough: areas on a golf course outside the fairways that feature higher, thicker grass or naturally growing vegetation

scooped: published a news story before a rival news reporter

sidebar: a short news story or graphic accompanying a longer newspaper or magazine article

siege: an operation where enemy forces surround a building with the aim of compelling the surrender of those inside

statistics: numerical data; in sports, an athlete's performance data

subjective: based on, or influenced by, personal feelings or opinions

sully: damage the integrity of someone or something (past tense: sullied)

thick skin: a quality that allows a person to be less sensitive to criticism or insults

ticker: information from telegraph wire transmission read by a sportscaster to recreate a game

underdog: a competitor who is thought to have less of a chance to win a contest

undergraduate: a student at a university or college who has not yet earned their bachelor's degree

Watergate: a political scandal in which an attempt to bug the national headquarters of the Democratic Party (in the Watergate building in Washington, DC) led to the resignation of President Nixon in 1974

Acknowledgments

COMPLETING ANY project under deadline is a difficult task without the help of others. I would like to thank the following individuals who helped me do so.

First and foremost, this biography would not have occurred without the cooperation and assistance of the subject, Christine, or as I've come to know her, Chris Brennan. She is amazing and went above and beyond. It was always fun learning where she was jetting off to next as I requested input, photos, and permissions from her.

I am forever indebted to the support of my husband, Brad, and our children, Kyle and Ian. They hold my hands when times are tough and dance with me when life is a bit easier. I am grateful too for the spirit and energy from our dear angel, Claire. This book is the last I will write in her precious space, and I appreciate her lending her inspiration to me. I have no doubt she will follow wherever I go.

I am grateful to the University of Florida and Forsyth Library for lending their images to Christine's story.

Thank you to the athletes whose stories are scattered throughout Christine's. It was a pleasure learning more about your accomplishments and challenges.

Thank you to my friends Amy and Laila, who have read through my first drafts and helped polish them up. You ladies are the best!

Series editor and friend Michelle Houts and copy editor Chiquita Babb have a fabulous way with my words. I am grateful for your efforts to make mine the best they could be.

Finally, thank you to the amazingly supportive staff at Ohio University Press. You have all given me the opportunity to shed light on yet another incredible writer for young readers. I am grateful beyond words.

Notes

Chapter One: In the Locker Room

1. Christine Brennan, "Christine Brennan, a Legendary Sports Journalist . . . in Her Own Words," interview, *Still No Cheering in the Press Box*, Shirley Povich Center for Sports Journalism, Philip Merrill College of Journalism, University of Maryland, https://povichcenter.org/still-no-cheering-press-box /chapter/Christine-Brennan/index.html.

2. Christine Brennan, *Best Seat in the House: A Father, a Daughter, a Journey through Sports* (New York: Scribner/Lisa Drew Books, 2006), 120.

3. Christine Brennan, interview in *Let Them Wear Towels*, documentary, directed by Ricki Stern and Annie Sundberg (New York: ESPN Films, Nine for IX series, 2013).

4. Brennan, *Best Seat in the House*, 120.

5. Ibid., 121.

6. *Let Them Wear Towels*.

7. Brennan, *Best Seat in the House*, 123.

8. *Let Them Wear Towels*.

Chapter Two: Drive

1. Christine Brennan, "Identifying Pathways to Promotion" (Women in Leadership Conference, Creating and Pursuing Pathways for Promotion, Bowling Green State University and University of Toledo, Perrysburg, OH, October 21, 2016).

2. "Political Hostess Put Family First," obituary of Betty Brennan, *Toledo Blade*, May 26, 2002, https://www.toledoblade.com/news/deaths/2002/05 /26/Political-hostess-put-family-first/sories/200205260046.

3. Fritz Wenzel, "Chairman Used Strong Hand in County's GOP," obituary of James Brennan, *Toledo Blade*, August 12, 2003, https://toledoblade .com/news/deaths/2003/08/12/Chairman-used-strong-hand-in-county-s -GOP/stories/200308120043.

4. "Political Hostess Put Family First."

5. Brennan, *Best Seat in the House,* 6.

6. Ibid., 7.

7. Ibid., 3.

8. Brennan, "Identifying Pathways to Promotion."

9. Brennan, *Best Seat in the House,* 11.

10. Ibid.

11. Ibid., 3.

12. Media Kit, *USA Today,* http://marketing.usatoday.com/about.

13. Brennan, *Best Seat in the House,* 15.

14. Ibid., 18

15. Brennan, "Identifying Pathways to Promotion."

16. Christine Brennan, interview in *Undefeated: The Chuck Ealey Story,* documentary, produced by Ray Miller (Toledo: WGTE, The Public Broadcasting Foundation of Northwest Ohio and C2 Land Productions, 2009), https://www.ohiochannel.org/programs/program/undefeated-the-chuck-ealey-story.

17. Brennan, *Best Seat in the House,* 38.

18. Brennan, *Undefeated: The Chuck Ealey Story.*

19. Larry Isle, interview in *Undefeated: The Chuck Ealey Story.*

20. Brennan, *Best Seat in the House,* 41.

Chapter Three: Box Out

1. Christine Brennan, University of Toledo winter commencement speech, December 20, 2008.

2. Brennan, *Best Seat in the House,* 92.

3. David Goldblatt, *The Games: A Global History of the Olympics* (New York: W. W. Norton, 2016), 285.

4. "Munich, Israel, Cleveland: Tragedy," *Cleveland Jewish News,* September 8, 1972.

5. Brennan, *Best Seat in the House,* 93.

6. Ibid., 94.

7. Brennan, "Identifying Pathways to Promotion."

8. Brennan, *Best Seat in the House,* 43.

9. Ibid., 54.

10. Ibid.

11. Ibid., 77.

12. Ibid., 75.

13. Susan Ware, *Game, Set, Match: Billie Jean King and the Revolution in Women's Sports*, (Chapel Hill: University of North Carolina Press, 2011), 1.

14. Ibid.

15. Christine Brennan, University of Toledo winter commencement speech.

16. Ed Wittenberg, "Olympics Honor David Berger, Munich 11—At Last," *Cleveland Jewish News*, August 10, 2016, https://www.clevelandjewishnews .com/news/local_news/olympics-honor-david-berger-munich-at-last/article _75835442-5f06-11e6-b304-274396331799.html.

Chapter Four: Rookie

1. Brennan, *Best Seat in the House*, 100.

2. Christine Brennan, telephone interview, March 12, 2018.

3. Brennan, *Best Seat in the House*, 99.

4. Ibid.

5. Megan McKinney, *The Magnificent Medills: America's Royal Family of Journalism During a Century of Turbulent Splendor* (New York: Harper Collins, 2011), 39.

6. Brennan, *Best Seat in the House*, 99.

7. Ibid., 100.

8. Ibid., 101.

9. Ibid., 110.

10. Ibid.

11. Ibid., 112.

Chapter Five: Unsportsmanlike Behavior

1. Brennan, Best Seat in the House, 126.

2. Brennan, telephone interview, March 12, 2018.

3. Ibid.

4. Brennan, "Identifying Pathways to Promotion."

5. Ibid.

6. "Christine Brennan, a Legendary Sports Journalist . . . in Her Own Words."

7. Betsy M. Ross, *Playing Ball with the Boys: The Rise of Women in the World of Men's Sports* (Covington, KY: Clerisy Press, 2010), 78.

8. Ibid.

9. Brennan, *Best Seat in the House*, 129.

10. "The Racial and Gender Report Card," The Institute for Diversity and Ethics in Sport, https://www.tidesport/racial-gender-report-card.org.

Chapter Six: Major Leagues

1. Christine Brennan, "Vox Populi," Politics and Prose Bookstore, http://www.politics-prose.com/vox-populi/christine-brennan.

2. "Michael Wilbon, a Legendary Sports Journalist . . . in His Own Words," *Still No Cheering in the Press Box,* https://povichcenter.org/still-no-cheering -press-box/chapter/Michael-Wilbon/index.html.

3. David Wallechinsky and Jaime Loucky, *The Complete Book of the Olympics: 2012 Edition* (London: Aurum Press, 2012), 23.

4. Brennan, *Best Seat in the House*, 179.

5. Christine Brennan, "Keeping Score: 25 Years Later, Olympic Boycott Gnaws at Athletes," *USA Today*, April 13, 2005, https://www.usatoday30.usatoday .com/sports/columnist/brennan/2005-04-13-brennan_x/html.

6. Ibid., 154.

7. Ibid., 155.

8. Ibid., 156.

Chapter Seven: Live from the Olympics

1. Brennan, *Best Seat in the House*, 182.

2. Franz Lidz, "Whatever Happened to Eddie the Eagle, Britain's Most Lovable Ski Jumper?," *Smithsonian*, February 2014, https://www.smithsonianmag .com/history/whatever-happened-to-eddie-eagle-britains-most-lovable-ski -jumper-180949438.

3. Lisa Albertson, H., *Seoul Calgary 1988: The Official Publication of the US Olympic Committee,* edited by John Robinson (Sandy, UT: Commemorative Publications, 1989), 12.

4. Brennan, *Best Seat in the House*, 182.

5. Albertson, *Seoul Calgary 1988*, 129.

6. Christine Brennan, "Louganis Takes Gold after Hitting Board," *Washington Post,* September 20, 1988, https://www.washingtonpost.com/archive

/politics/1988/09/20/louganis-takes-gold-after-hitting-board/e21ca740-5ab8
-4cc4-b0cd-49b73fbd95db/.

7. Brennan, *Best Seat in the House*, 183.

8. Ken Porter and Ron Wilson, broadcasters, "Ben Johnson: A Hero Disgraced," *CBC Rewind,* Canadian Broadcast System, CBC Olympics, September 24, 1988, https://www.cbc.ca/sports/olympics/trackandfield/ben-johnson
-a-hero-disgraced-1.1860203.

9. Brennan, *Best Seat in the House*, 184.

10. *Nancy and Tonya,* documentary (New York: NBC Sports, 2014), https://sportsworld.nbcsports.com/nancy-tonya/.

11. *30 for 30: The Price of Gold*, documentary, directed by Nanette Burstein (New York: ESPN Films, 2014).

12. Bruce Horovitz, "Going for the Gold: Advertisers Race to Sign Olympic Medalists," *Los Angeles Times,* March 1, 1994, articles.latimes.com/1994-03
-01/business/fi-28637_1_gold-medal.

13. Tom Van Riper, "What It Costs to Raise a Winter Olympian," *Forbes,* February 1, 2010, https:// www.forbes.com/2010/01/28/winter-olympics-training
-costs-business-sportsmoney-olympic-champs.html#39a49e82cd6b.

Chapter Eight: Figure Skating

1. Brennan, *Best Seat in the House*, 190.

2. Alexander Abad-Santos, "A GIF Guide to Figure Skaters' Jumps at the Olympics," *Atlantic,* February 5, 2014, https://www.the atlantic.com
/entertainment/archive/2014/02/gif-guide-figure-skaters-jumps-olympics
/357723.

Chapter Nine: Going National

1. Brennan, *Best Seat in the House*, 201.

2. Media Kit, *USA Today,* https://marketing.usatoday.com/about.

3. Christine Brennan, interviewed in "Christine Brennan, Sports Columnist and TV Commentator," *Our Town with Andy Ockershausen,* January 21, 2017, http://ourtowndc.com/christine-brennan-sports/.

4. David Owen, *The Making of the Masters: Clifford Roberts, Augusta National, and Golf's Most Prestigious Tournament* (New York: Simon & Schuster, 1999), 14.

5. Brennan, *Best Seat in the House,* 237.

6. Ibid., 238.

7. Christine Brennan, "Finally! Augusta Does Right Thing and Admits Women," *USA Today,* August 20, 2012, https://www.usatoday.com/sports/golf/masters/story/2012-08-20/Masters-women-Condoleeza-Rice-Darla-Moore-Christine-Brennan/57160258/1.

8. Christine Brennan, "Skating Insiders Question Sochi Gold Judging," *USA Today,* February 20, 2014, https://www.usatoday.com/story/sports/columnist/brennan/2014/02/20/winter-olympics-games-sochi-figure-skating-women-yuna-kim-gracie-gold/5643143/.

9. Christine Brennan, "NFL Owners Turn Blind Eye on Domestic Violence," October 26, 2016, https://www.usatoday.com/story/sports/columnist/brennan/2016/10/26/josh-brown-john-mara-new-york-giants-ray-rice/92791240/.

10. Ibid.

11. Ibid.

12. Christine Brennan, "Ryan Lochte Owes Rio, Olympics an Apology," *USA Today,* August 18, 2016, https://www.usatoday.com/story/sports/columnist/brennan/2016/08/18/brennan-ryan-lochte-owes-rio-olympics-apology/88969856/.

13. Christine Brennan, phone interview, February 21, 2017.

14. "Christine Brennan, a Legendary Sportswriter . . .in Her Own Words."

15. Brennan, phone interview, February 21, 2017.

16. Christine Brennan, "Powerful Mean Tweets PSA Years in the Making," *USA Today,* April 27, 2016, https://www.usatoday.com/story/sports/columnist/brennan/2016/04/27/brennan-powerful-psa-mean-tweets-years-making/83620310.

17. Ibid.

Chapter Ten: Passing the Baton

1. Terry Oberle, "North Carolinian First Woman to Win Associated Press Sports Editors Highest Honor," *Associated Press Sports Editors,* July 14, 2005, Apsportseditors.com/mary-garber.

2. Christine Brennan, University of Toledo commencement speech, May 7, 2017, www.utoledo.edu.

3. Christine Brennan, lecture, "Must See Sports: Christine Brennan," Walter Cronkite School of Journalism and Mass Communication, Arizona State

University, Phoenix, January 29, 2015, https://cronkite.asu.edu/news-and-events
/events/speaker-series/must-see-sports-christine-brennan.

4. Ibid.

5. Ibid.

6. Brennan, University of Toledo winter commencement speech.

7. Sue Macy, *"Miss Mary Reporting: The True Story of Sportswriter Mary
Garber,"* illustrated by C. F. Payne (New York: Simon & Schuster/Paula Wiseman Books, 2016), 10.

8. Christine Brennan, speech, "Authors! Authors!" *Toledo Blade* and the
Toledo Lucas County Public Library, Toledo, OH, April 1996, www.toledolibrary
.org/authors.

Bibliography

Books

Albertson, Lisa H. *Seoul Calgary 1988: The Official Publication of the US Olympic Committee.* Edited by John Robinson. Sandy, UT: Commemorative Publications, 1989.

Brennan, Christine. *Best Seat in the House: A Father, a Daughter, a Journey through Sports.* New York: Scribner/Lisa Drew Books, 2006.

———. *Champions on Ice.* New York: McClelland & Stewart, 2002.

———. *Edge of Glory: The Inside Story of the Quest for Figure Skating's Olympic Gold Medals.* New York: Scribner, 2013.

———. *Inside Edge: A Revealing Journey into the Secret World of Figure Skating.* New York: Scribner/Lisa Drew Books, 1996.

Gitlin, Marty. *Florida Gators.* Inside College Football series. Minneapolis: ABDO Publishing, 2013.

Goldblatt, David. *The Games: A Global History of the Olympics.* New York: W. W. Norton, 2016.

Macy, Sue. *Miss Mary Reporting: The True Story of Sportswriter Mary Garber.* Illustrated by C. F. Payne. New York: Simon & Schuster/Paula Wiseman Books, 2016.

Nardo, Don. *Massacre in Munich: How Terrorists Changed the Olympics and the World.* North Mankato, MN: Compass Point Books/Capstone, 2016.

McKinney, Megan. *The Magnificent Medills: America's Royal Family of Journalism During a Century of Turbulent Splendor.* New York: HarperCollins, 2011.

Owen, David. *The Making of the Masters: Clifford Roberts, Augusta National, and Golf's Most Prestigious Tournament.* New York: Simon & Schuster, 1999.

Rappaport, Ken. *Ladies First: Women Athletes Who Made a Difference.* Atlanta: Peachtree Publishers, 2005.

Ross, Betsy M. *Playing Ball with the Boys: The Rise of Women in the World of Men's Sports.* Covington, KY: Clerisy Press, 2010.

Wallechinsky, David, and Jaime Loucky. *The Complete Book of the Olympics: 2012 Edition*. London: Aurum Press, 2012.

Ware, Susan. *Game, Set, Match: Billie Jean King and the Revolution in Women's Sports*. Chapel Hill: University of North Carolina Press, 2011.

Articles

Author unknown. "Munich, Israel, Cleveland: Tragedy." *Cleveland Jewish News*, September 8, 1972.

Author unknown. "Political Hostess Put Family First." Obituary of Betty Brennan. *Toledo Blade*, May 26, 2002. https://www.toledoblade.com/news/deaths/2002/05/26/Political-hostess-put-family-first/stories/200205260046.

Abad-Santos, Alexander. "A GIF Guide to Figure Skaters' Jumps at the Olympics." *Atlantic*, February 5, 2014. https://www.the atlantic.com/entertainment/archive/2014/02/gif-guide-figure-skaters-jumps-olympics/357723.

Brennan, Christine. "Christine Brennan, a Legendary Sports Journalist . . . in Her Own Words." *Still No Cheering in the Press Box*. Shirley Povich Center for Sports Journalism, Philip Merrill College of Journalism, University of Maryland. https://povichcenter.org/still-no-cheering-press-box/chapter/Christine-Brennan/index.html.

————. "Everything Happens So Fast." *Washington Post*, January 7, 1996. http://www.washingtonpost.com/archive/lifestyle/magazine/1996/01/07/everything-happens-so-fast/7c60a4cb-f5ce-4ba5-80ac-5a33589722eb/?utm_term=.dc2091f45665.

————. "Finally! Augusta Does Right Thing and Admits Women." *USA Today*, August 20, 2012. https://www.usatoday.com/sports/golf/masters/story/2012-08-20/Masters-women-Condoleeza-Rice-Darla-Moore-Christine-Brennan/57160258/1.

————. "IOC Strips Johnson of Gold Medal in 100." *Washington Post*, September 27, 1988. http://www.washingtonpost.com/archive/politics/1988/09/27/ioc-strips-johnson-of-gold-medal-in-100/9cd59877-87c4-44ec-9e98-69eb58f37fa2.

————. "Keeping Score: 25 Years Later, Olympic Boycott Gnaws at Athletes." *USA Today*, April 13, 2005. https://www.usatoday30.usatoday.com/sports/columnist/brennan/2005-04-13-brennan_x/html.

————. "Louganis Takes Gold after Hitting Board." *Washington Post*, September 20, 1988. https://www.washingtonpost.com/archive/politics/1988

/09/20/louganis-takes-gold-after-hitting-board/e21ca740-5ab8-4cc4
-b0cd-49b73fbd95db/.

———. "NFL Owners Turn Blind Eye on Domestic Violence." October 26, 2016. https://www.usatoday.com/story/sports/columnist/brennan/2016 /10/26/josh-brown-john-mara-new-york-giants-ray-rice/92791240/.

———. "Powerful Mean Tweets PSA Years in the Making." *USA Today*, April 27, 2016. https://www.usatoday.com/story/sports/columnist/brennan/2016 /04/27/brennan-powerful-psa-mean-tweets-years-making/83620310.

———. "Ryan Lochte Owes Rio, Olympics an Apology." *USA Today*, August 18, 2016. https://www.usatoday.com/story/sports/columnist/brennan/2016 /08/18/brennan-ryan-lochte-owes-rio-olympics-apology/88969856/.

———. "Skating Insiders Question Sochi Gold Judging." *USA Today*, February 20, 2014. https://www.usatoday.com/story/sports/columnist/brennan /2014/02/20/winter-olympics-games-sochi-figure-skating-women-yuna -kim-gracie-gold/5643143/.

Goldstein, Richard. "Mary Garber, Sportswriter, Dies at 92." *New York Times*, September 22, 2008. https://www.nytimes.com/2008/09/23/sports/23garber /html.

Horovitz, Bruce. "Going for the Gold: Advertisers Race to Sign Olympic Medalists." *Los Angeles Times,* March 1, 1994. articles.latimes.com/1994-03-01 /business/fi-28637_1_gold-medal.

Lidz, Franz. "Whatever Happened to Eddie the Eagle, Britain's Most Lovable Ski Jumper?" *Smithsonian*, February 2014. https://www.smithsonianmag. com/history/whatever-happened-to-eddie-eagle-britains-most-lovable -ski-jumper-180949438.

Oberle, Terry. "North Carolinian First Woman to Win Associated Press Sports Editors Highest Honor." *Associated Press Sports Editors*, July 14, 2005. Apsportseditors.com/mary-garber/.

Rosewater, Amy, and Lynn Rutherford. "Weiss Finds Greatest Joy in Giving Back." Special to *icenetwork.com*, October 3, 2011.

Van Riper, Tom. "What It Costs to Raise a Winter Olympian." *Forbes*, February 1, 2010. https:// www.forbes.com/2010/01/28/winter-olympics-training -costs-business-sportsmoney-olympic-champs.html#39a49e82cd6b.

Wenzel, Fritz. "Chairman Used Strong Hand in County's GOP." Obituary of James Brennan. *Toledo Blade*, August 12, 2003. https://toledoblade .com/news/deaths/2003/08/12/Chairman-used-strong-hand-in-county -s-GOP/stories/200308120043.

Wilbon, Michael. "Michael Wilbon, a Legendary Sports Journalist . . . in His Own Words." *Still No Cheering in the Press Box*. Shirley Povich Center for

Sports Journalism, Philip Merrill College of Journalism, University of Maryland. https://povichcenter.org/still-no-cheering-press-box/chapter/Michael-Wilbon/index.html.

Wittenberg, Ed. "Olympics Honor David Berger, Munich 11—At Last." *Cleveland Jewish News*, August 10, 2016. https://www.clevelandjewishnews.com/news/local_news/olympics-honor-david-berger-munich-at-last/article_75835442-5f06-11e6-b304-274396331799.html.

Websites

APSE (Associate Press Sports Editors). www.apsportseditors.com.

Ice Network. www.icenetwork.com.

Miami Herald. www.miamiherald.com.

New York Times. www.nytimes.com.

Politics and Prose Bookstore. www.politics-prose.com.

Pro Football Hall of Fame. www.profootballhof.com.

The Shirley Povich Center for Sports Journalism. www.povichcenter.org.

Toledo Blade. www.toledoblade.com.

University of Miami. www.welcomemiami.edu.

USA Today. www.usatoday.com.

Walter Cronkite School of Journalism and Mass Communications, Arizona State University, Phoenix. www.cronkite.asu.edu.

Washington Post. www.washingtonpost.com.

Audio

Porter, Ken, and Ron Wilson, broadcasters. "Ben Johnson: A Hero Disgraced." *CBC Rewind.* Canadian Broadcast System, CBC Sports Olympics, September 24, 1988. www.cbc.ca/sports/olympics/trackandfield/ben-johnson-a-hero-disgraced-1.1860203.

Podcast

"Christine Brennan, Sports Columnist and TV Commentator." Interview. *Our Town with Andy Ockershausen.* January 21, 2017. http://ourtowndc.com/christine-brennan-sports/.

Film

Let Them Wear Towels. Documentary. Directed by Ricki Stern and Annie Sundberg. New York: ESPN Films, Nine for IX series, 2013.

Nancy and Tonya. Documentary. New York: NBC Sports, 2014. https://sportsworld.nbcsports.com/nancy-tonya/.

Undefeated: The Chuck Ealey Story. Documentary. Produced by Ray Miller. Toledo: WGTE, The Public Broadcasting Foundation of Northwest Ohio and C2 Land Productions, 2009. https://www.ohiochannel.org/programs/program/undefeated-the-chuck-ealey-story.

30 for 30: The Price of Gold. Documentary. Directed by Nanette Burstein. New York: ESPN Films, 2014.

Interviews

Brennan, Christine. Personal interview, October 21, 2016. Phone interviews, February 21, 2017, and March 12, 2018. Various email correspondences.

Lectures/Speeches

Brennan, Christine. "Authors! Authors!" *Toledo Blade* and the Toledo Lucas County Public Library, Toledo, OH. April 1996. www.toledolibrary.org/authors.

———. "Identifying Pathways to Promotion." Women in Leadership Conference, Creating and Pursuing Pathways for Promotion, Bowling Green State University and University of Toledo, Perrysburg, Ohio, October 21, 2016.

———. University of Toledo commencement speech, May 7, 2017.

———. University of Toledo winter commencement speech, December 20, 2008.

———. "Must See Sports: Christine Brennan." Walter Cronkite School of Journalism and Mass Communication, Arizona State University, Phoenix, January 29, 2015. https://cronkite.asu.edu/news-and-events/events/speaker-series/must-see-sports-christine-brennan.